D1564884

CHINESE PRODIGAL

CHINESE PRODIGAL

A MEMOIR IN EIGHT ARGUMENTS

DAVID SHIH

Atlantic Monthly Press
New York

For the poem featured on page 256: Lai, Him Mark, Genny Lim, and Judy Yung, eds. *Island: Poetry and History of Chinese Immigrants on Angel Island, 1910–1940*. pp. 84–85. © 1991. Reprinted with permission of the University of Washington Press.

FIRST EDITION

Published simultaneously in Canada
Printed in the United States of America

This book was set in 11.2-pt. Berling LT
by Alpha Design & Composition of Pittsfield, NH.

First Grove Atlantic hardcover edition: August 2023

Library of Congress Cataloging-in-Publication data is available for this title.

ISBN 978-0-8021-5899-4
eISBN 978-0-8021-5900-7

Atlantic Monthly Press
an imprint of Grove Atlantic
154 West 14th Street
New York, NY 10011

Distributed by Publishers Group West

groveatlantic.com

23 24 25 26   10 9 8 7 6 5 4 3 2 1

for my parents

If the relationship of father to son could really be reduced to biology, the whole earth would blaze with the glory of fathers and sons.

James Baldwin, *The Devil Finds Work*

CONTENTS

CONTENTS

CHINESE PRODIGAL

INTRODUCTION

The idea for *Chinese Prodigal* began shortly after my father passed away in 2019. I was living in Wisconsin when it happened, as I still do, and I couldn't make it back home to Texas before he died in the hospital. I had about two weeks. What took me so long? That was the big question I set out to explore in the title chapter and, less pointedly, in the others. The easy answer, which is not entirely inaccurate, is that I was self-absorbed and uncaring, a bad son. But I'd like to believe that nothing about family is so simple. In this book, I sought to plumb the nature of the relationship between a Chinese immigrant father and his son, an immigrant himself, but one who had spent all but a year of his life in the United States.

What did it matter, for instance, that we left Hong Kong and came to this country in 1971 under the auspices of the 1965 Hart-Celler Act, which ended decades of racist policy that had effectively banned immigration from

Asia? What did it matter that I excelled at my studies as a child, mastering English at the expense of Chinese, and not only stopped needing my parents' guidance in grade school but actively began to distrust it? What did it matter that I found myself in largely segregated educational, professional, and residential spaces, most of my own choosing, well into adulthood and a parenthood of my own? These questions seemed to take me far afield from the one I'd set out to answer, and I hoped that they were not mine alone.

What I needed to explore was race, namely its covert reaches into my life and into those of the people and institutions that saw me in racial terms whether they knew it or not. But my efforts weren't focused exclusively on figuring out what others thought was good or bad or tolerable about being Chinese or Asian in the United States but also on determining how those meanings depended on the state of being white and Black at any given moment. I wanted to understand how "Asian American" identity was invented and reinvented in the wake of the civil rights movement and later historical struggles for racial justice for Black Americans. Although I wasn't aware of the term "model minority" until I was an adult, the idea behind it—that I was deserving not just because I was Asian but because I wasn't Black— no doubt opened doors and hearts to me in ways that I wasn't aware had anything to do with race. I grew up in the seventies and eighties, a time when the significance of Asian-ness was still being hashed out, whether in the anxious chatter over Nixon's visit to the People's Republic of China or in the bad faith dialogues of American supporters of the Vietnam War. So many of the survivors of that war— the refugees from South Vietnam, Laos, and Cambodia, I mean—would become Asian Americans like me, although none of us thought about ourselves that way at the time. In my mind, my story had already diverged from theirs, and it was a story of difference and supremacy over them that I told as an adolescent jockeying for status between Black and white. I didn't know or want to know what I might have in common with these peers, which was, of course, race and the very reason we might be mistaken for one another.

In time, I began to think about myself and others in healthier ways. I learned in graduate school that race was a social construct, an idea and a reality meant to preserve the highest social status for white Americans, usually by defining the contours of Blackness—in law, in popular culture, and in education. What Asian identity reveals about the system of racism is just how unstable this idea of race is, because over the course of our time in the United States, beginning in the mid-nineteenth century, Asians such as the Chinese and Japanese have had the meanings of our bodies and communities and deeds change and even reverse along with

3

the vicissitudes of geopolitical affairs. The Asian American of Generation X is old enough to have lived through many of these permutations, whose stereotypes would ensure or endanger our safety and success, tempting all of us to tweak our bodies and behaviors on the fly. Communist. Anti-Communist. Refugee. Sex worker. Entrepreneur. Viet Cong. Valedictorian. Doctor. Naturalized citizen. Honorary white. Welfare charge. Tiger mom. China virus. Spy. If we can stand in for so many things at so many times, what can "Asian American" even mean or hope to accomplish as an identity and a creed? I sought the answer to that question too. It was inextricable from what I'd hoped to learn about the nature of my prodigality, especially with the one resource that mattered the most, time.

* * *

When I was growing up, nobody I knew said "Asian American." The only words we had to talk about Asians were "Chinese" and "Japanese." "Vietnamese" in some circles, but only because of the war. I knew about the Japanese because white people in my life still said "Jap" like a regular word and because of my fascination with World War II. I was relieved not to be Japanese. In the fifth grade, we were asked to dress up as Americans famous for their speeches, and I chose Douglas MacArthur. I cracked open the Funk & Wagnalls encyclopedias that my mother had assembled a volume at a time by redeeming supermarket prize stamps. I stared at the photo of the taciturn general with a mix of fear and admiration. My father, who loved MacArthur, helped me to make a fake corncob pipe, and I stuck a circle of five gold foil stars onto a royal-blue Members Only jacket. Even as a kid I knew that the pipe and insignia were critical props to compensate for my face. I may have worn sunglasses too. I stood in front of my class and recounted the tale of MacArthur's famous retreat from the Japanese at Corregidor and his pledge not to abandon his troops and the Filipino people. At the time, I didn't think about Filipinos as Asians like the Chinese and Japanese, although Filipinos knew before either what it meant to be this country's enemy. "I shall return," I said in my best whiteface, the first time I was happy not to be a Jap in public. The next year, I soured on MacArthur after learning about his being fired by President Truman, whom I admired for showing the courage to drop the bomb. I didn't know then that MacArthur had been recalled for wanting to kill more Koreans—also not yet Asians in my mind—and Chinese, a lot more, maybe by dropping the bomb too, and I probably would have trusted his judgment over Truman's like the rest of the nation at the time if I had known that. I was led to assume that wars made it easy for white Americans to tell the difference among all the Asian people they had killed.

I was wrong. I was thinking along the lines of nation and ethnicity, which may have worked to tell us who we were in Asia, although less so in colonial or neocolonial settings like South Korea, South Vietnam, and Hong Kong, where I was born. But the moment we crossed the border into this country—whether because of a decision that was economic like my parents' or existential like those of the Vietnamese, Cambodians, and Hmong—we were assigned a race as well, painted with the broad brush of "Asian" or "Oriental" and all its attendant connotations by those who didn't have to know the difference in their lives, which was mostly everyone. I crawled against this tide of racist homogenization that might take the form of cultural curiosity ("What's in sukiyaki?") or outright intimidation ("Are you Viet Cong?"), but I rarely made much headway. It was because I was engaging on the terms of my interlocutors, who were usually white, doing my best to explain how the Chinese were different from the Japanese or the Vietnamese, when, in truth, all I wanted was for the conversation to end with their assent that I was much more like them than like anyone else. They were the final arbiters of my belonging, and that was because their terms didn't include talking about the one thing that might tip the scales and put them on the defensive, which, I know now, has always been anti-Blackness.

For in addition to being painted with the broad brush of the "Asian" or "Oriental" race, so too were many of us washed with the racial identity of "not Black," which is not the same as white, even though some of us hoped it was. There are degrees of truth to this statement, no doubt, beginning with the Filipinos abandoned by MacArthur and then the Vietnamese, Cambodians, and Hmong abandoned by his successors. But if we were required to define, as pithily and as accurately as possible, what it meant to be "Asian American" (or, in my case, one of its anachronistic cognates: "American Chinese," "American of Chinese descent," "overseas Chinese," etc.), we could do far worse than "not Black." I suppose that dropping that term into heritage-month colloquies about the meaning of "Asian American" or "Chinese American" or "Japanese American" would be considered cheating by the earnest organizers of such events. But it is not; it is, in fact, its opposite, which is honesty. Just as our nation has immorally bookended Black and white to enrich itself, so too has it schemed the places of Black and Asian for the ongoing benefit of white supremacy. To the white people in my life who were the kindest to me, very often the ones who told me that they didn't think about me as Chinese, I wondered if I ever seemed like a visitor from the near future, an alien who could speak and laugh and love like them and never once remind them of their near past that could not recede quickly enough.

* * *

For the last twenty years, I've been a professor of English at a regional midwestern university, which seems to make sense given my youthful desire for assimilation and my capacity for consuming the vital but underexamined stories of our culture. A less predictable outcome is that I am a specialist in the field of Asian American literature, bringing the American stories of writers and artists of Asian ancestry to my students. Certain key insights from those writers and artists are sprinkled throughout *Chinese Prodigal*. A small number of my students are Asian American but the vast majority are not, unlike in the University of California system or the Ivy League. To my colleagues who hired me and my students who register for my classes, my job must seem pretty straightforward: diversify the curriculum by sharing the stories about what it means to be Asian American. No doubt everyone in my classes learns about or learns more about the historical events around which so many of these stories revolve: the Chinese Exclusion Act, Japanese American incarceration, Indian independence, the Korean War, the Hart-Celler Act, the Vietnam War, the Secret War in Laos, Vincent Chin, the Los Angeles riots or uprising. They encounter the broad humanity of the people making a life under such circumstances, perhaps learning a little something about resilience and grace to put away for themselves. These are important takeaways. And yet I feel as though the course's potential is unfulfilled if these stories don't lead my students to think about themselves even more deeply than they ponder the protagonists, not how they might relate to them but how they don't and why. Here my job is less straightforward, because it is to show how racism dwindles one's choices for how to experience life—where we might work and reside, what we might speak and how, whom we might know and love—pushing some options just beyond consciousness or the realm of possibility. I ought to know.

Chinese Prodigal is the story of those options coalescing before me, slowly, some a little too late to avoid a durable regret. After decades of sharing my ideas with thousands of students, so many of them continuing inspirations, I wanted to try to write them down to see if I could do it. I wanted to see if I could put my English education, that pearl of great price, to work—to make it serve as more than just a credential. I didn't think my first book would come so belatedly in my career, but now I hope I know why. These days I keep a slip of paper taped to my computer monitor with a quotation I like. The words belong to James

Baldwin. A few years before his death, Baldwin was asked by an interviewer what experience had taught him about writing. "You learn how little you know," he replied. "It becomes much more difficult because the hardest thing in the world is simplicity. And the most fearful thing, too. It becomes more difficult because you have to strip yourself of all your disguises, some of which you didn't know you had. You want to write a sentence as clean as a bone. That is the goal." I took him to mean that your bad writing told on you, because to be a coherent writer is to know who you are, which comes with facing down your fears. The tendency to not do that, to not face down your fears and know who you are, is a peculiarly American dishonesty, Baldwin knew, which explains why it was a part of my life for so long. The fear is nothing more than that of being exposed as a fraud and then losing something because of that reckoning, or many things, beginning with that deep sense of yourself as a hard worker or an ardent lover or a genuine American or an honest-to-goodness pilgrim, all those disguises you had read about at one point or another and maybe thought to try on.

But the meaning of *Chinese Prodigal*, ultimately, must come from someone other than me. In this way, a book is like a race: it appears to have essential meaning in and of itself, but that meaning has always been authored by the one who regards it. I had to learn how to *read* a sentence as clean as a bone too, spurning the sophistry of others as well as my own slanted interpretations that would preserve a fiction of superiority, or rationality, or innocence. There is always something precious at stake for us in the meanings we allow to prevail, first in our minds and then in our actions. Reading is fighting.

It stands to reason that one of my favorite books to teach is *The Woman Warrior: Memoirs of a Girlhood among Ghosts*, by Maxine Hong Kingston. In its most famous chapter, Kingston restyles the story of the famed warrior Fa Mu Lan, who razors the grievances of the poor and oppressed into her flesh. "What we have in common are the words at our backs," she writes. "The idioms for *revenge* are 'report a crime' and 'report to five families.' The reporting is the vengeance—not the beheading, not the gutting, but the words. And I have so many words—'chink' words and 'gook' words too—that they do not fit on my skin." We imagine ourselves into Asian Americans by reading and writing the best words and the worst.

Like me, the Chinese American Kingston grew up condescending to her immigrant parents, at one point arguing fiercely with her mother, Brave Orchid, before leaving home for college and a life beyond her family. As a girl, Kingston felt trapped by her perception of a misogynistic Chinese culture, which threatened to leave her no option but assimilation to American institutions. Brave Orchid tried to inspire her by telling her the story of Fa Mu Lan, a girl who saved her village. "I could not figure out what was my village," the young Maxine laments. "Asian American" identity as we know it now was not a possibility, and she had not yet been to China. In 1984, as part of a delegation of American writers invited to visit Beijing by their Chinese counterparts, Kingston took the opportunity to seek out her ancestral village, whose dialect is different from those of other parts of Guangdong Province. Joined by fellow American writers Toni Morrison and Leslie Marmon Silko, she floated down the Li River, trying out her dialect with the locals until she found a match. Kingston had found the right words for the right audience at the right time, thereby claiming, at last, the true inheritance her mother had wanted her to have.

We should all be so lucky.

CHAPTER 1
CHINESE PRODIGAL

When we lost my father that night in the hospital, it had been almost two weeks since a stroke dropped him flat in the house he had occupied for almost half his life and whose simple comforts he had pleaded with his family to return him to in his final days. It was a redbrick ranch, one of thousands churned out by a builder who marketed tract homes like Chevys to young families in the booming north Dallas suburbs of the seventies. Ours was the deluxe model of its modest line, which added a fourth bedroom and a wet bar, the latter an ironic choice given how seldom my parents entertained in later years. But they saw themselves differently in the world then, and this was their first house on any continent. Dad was almost forty-five years old when he could boast that he owned his own home—or that the "bank owned his own home," a joke that he told in English and that never failed to kill among my immigrant relatives. Back then, my parents didn't much resemble our neighbors but shared their optimism for the future, anchored by these homes that, even if not as stately or finely crafted as the custom numbers a few streets over, were at least as new as a morning star. For why would you uproot your people only to haunt a stranger's old domain? The house, I know now, was a solution to the problem of apartments and a growing family, imperfect but durable, a concrete reminder of your blood commitments.

Dad was like that with adversity. How he solved a problem may not have been ideal, but the option of doing nothing never occurred to him. The bank saddled my parents with a usurious mortgage, but we three kids at last had our own bedrooms, so exotic a setup at first that my older sister, Selma, and I, used to idly chatting at lights out, now took turns shouting at the thin drywall between us. When I was a teenager, Dad still did chores like mowing the lawn, because he didn't want to wait for me to wake up. He also spoiled me to the limit of his means, which, even as a child, I knew had to do with being Chinese. None of his three younger brothers had a son, and Dad welcomed their deference and jealousy when, out of the blue, one of them would grin at him and begin to chant, "First-born son, first-born son," clapping me hard on the shoulder with each syllable. I was the solution to another problem, one inherited like a debt: that of maintaining the family line.

The only problem my father didn't attend to with any urgency was his health. He hated going to the doctor and rarely did before he was eligible for Medicare. After he was diagnosed with type 2 diabetes at age sixty-nine, however, he was good about the maintenance. Over the Thanksgiving holiday that year, on my annual return to the house, he trailed me from room to room, waving his lancet and clamoring to test my blood, but I refused.

Because of his health and what I meant to him, you would have expected me to beat a path home after the first alarming text from my little sister, Teresa, the thousand miles between us a nonfactor, even if I had to drive, which of course I didn't. Instead, over those thirteen days, I threw a baby shower for colleagues, taught all but a few of my classes, shuttled my son to and from his after-school activities, FaceTimed with Dad when he wasn't sedated, read a new novel, watched premium cable with my wife in bed, and, at the tail end of that stretch, booked a flight to Dallas–Fort Worth International Airport that turned out to be a couple of days too late. There was no secret horror from the past between my father and me that would explain my procrastination, nothing so tidy that your curious friends would know exactly what you meant when you let slip, "We weren't close." I knew that I didn't inherit my father's initiative to take care of business, but I didn't expect my passivity to manifest itself in an affair of this order. Although I've tried to own the fault entirely, accepting my inaction as nothing but an abject moral failure, I don't think that take tells the whole story either, although it's likely a lot closer to the truth than I want it to be. The answer isn't to be found buried like a single bad memory or unshared principle between two men but spread out somewhere in the open, on public property. In a village, say. The answer has something to do, I've concluded since my father's death, with how one of these men learned what it means to be Chinese, and a son and a citizen besides.

*   *   *

My father treated work like a series of trials to overcome or at least outlast in between bits of downtime at that indispensable house. My parents owned a small wholesaling business that sold reproductions of antique Chinese export porcelain. My mother, whose English was better, ran the office. Dad was the traveling salesman, and it was the journeys embarking from the house that inspired the hopes and dreads we associated with his work. He drove a truck packed with samples of our wares to trade shows across the South. Houston was the closest, then Memphis, New Orleans, Atlanta—all the way out to North Carolina. He could be gone for weeks at a time if one show followed on the heels of another. Dad left before dawn to cover the familiar legs in the dark, rolling into his motor lodge in Metairie or Marietta while it was still light out. We kids roused to see him off, the white cube van already fired up and rumbling right there on our sleepy residential street, its yellow running lights aglow, the hardware-store black vinyl stickers on the door—SHIH & CO., INC.—barely legible. For good luck, Teresa handed over poster board signs markered up with well-wishes like DRIVE SAFELY AND MAKE LOTS OF $$$. Mom had prepped the big Igloo cooler that rode shotgun in the cab, filled halfway with the crescent-shaped ice that was spat from our refrigerator and on top of that the French baguettes, cubed cheese, and cases of Coke that none of us knew were beginning to wreck Dad's blood sugar. Selma and I usually didn't offer anything of our own, old enough now to consider our interrupted sleep sufficient tribute, but still we embraced him as if he were a GI embarking upon a tour of duty, one not without consequence or peril.

If there's any comfort to be taken from my father's death, it's that at least it was natural, one that probably could have been deferred with more attention paid to his needs by him and then by the hospital staff, but also one that had allowed for an ample lifetime, certainly above average. As a kid, I sometimes feared the worst when he was gone for an especially long time. The way he had to make a living struck me as a little unfair, anachronistic for its risk. The most predictable danger was falling asleep at the wheel, which Dad did many times, in one case abruptly slicing the cube van through the rough shoulder and then skippering it into the grassy ditch of median beyond, blowing out a few tires and requiring a tow back to Dallas. Dad was unhurt. But then more sinister threats surfaced once you arrived in the city or, more accurately, just as you were about to leave it, your briefcase stuffed with envelopes full of large bills from the final day's sample sales. Some of the Iranian gold and diamond dealers hired private security to escort them to their cars. Immigrants were especially inviting marks because they tended to be less talkative with police, owing to language barriers as well as the eventuality of having to report how much cash, exactly, had been stolen. Dealing with law enforcement and then the IRS was like a descent into consecutive hells for these men, and to set out down this path voluntarily usually meant you were already ruined.

In my early twenties, I spent a few summers traveling with my father, partly to help with the grunt work at shows—he was sixty by then—but also because I would be leaving Texas soon, for graduate school and then maybe for good. We arrived a couple of days before the show to set up, ahead of most other exhibitors. Dad still insisted on doing the heavy labor himself, I found, assembling the planks of splintery plywood shelving or steering a dolly from the loading dock across the convention center floor, crates stacked so high I saw only the top of his head as the boxy mass glided toward our booth. He allowed me to unpack crates and stock shelves and tables with samples, light tasks my mother would have assumed if she had been there. Dad never paced himself, his dark polo shirt inevitably streaked with white sweat stains by the end of the first day. At these moments I would ask him if he wanted to finish the rest tomorrow. "Let's get it over with it, huh?" was his usual reply, his twist on a favorite idiom. He had this ethic in common with the other exhibitors from Asia, and also from the Middle East, I noticed, some past middle age like himself. Young white people also worked hard, setting up for their bosses, older white exhibitors who flew in the night before the show. The next morning, I observed them in their booths chatting away with their customers, chuckling as if they were old friends they hadn't seen in a year. The talking seemed to be the work for them.

Perhaps because he had known them for years, Dad was friendly with the white men who owned these shows, and he wanted me to see him palling around with them whenever they cruised the floor of the convention hall. But he was more comfortable riffing with the Black men who unloaded the trucks and wired the booths, always sure to ask about their mothers and children. He hired locals to help write orders during show days, preferring genteel white women familiar with the interior design of the area's colonial mansions. Around them, Dad could be genuinely charming, even flirtatious, although nothing scandalous could ever brew between them. This was still Dixie, and Dad still that Oriental gentleman who just happened to be friendlier and more of a character than the other foreigners. They taught him how to flatter southern women like themselves to drum up sales, counsel he absorbed as articles of faith. These women represented the limits of his amity, ringing the outer bounds of his social circle. Going through boxes of old photos after he died, I found many of him in front of the booth with them, more than I'd expected, the slight variations in their respective hairstyles and fashions marking off the years like a series of Christmas cards.

I think my father came to depend on how these shows operated like little fiefdoms, more or less insulated from the city mandarins and run like a large family with big and little bosses, personal favors, cash sales, and no union labor. His favorite line was "I'll take care of you, okay?" which he used like punctuation to end a conversation, usually with the setup crew and electricians, slipping tens and twenties into their palms after they hooked him up with an extra display table or outlet. He must have liked the paternal feeling of it all, getting both the last word and the proper gratitude of a younger man. In turn, when he required the reach of executive power—perhaps to lean on another exhibitor whose booth encroached too far into his own space—he might collar a navy-suited young woman with a walkie-talkie and flip the script. "Take care of me, okay?" he would say at the end of their brief chat, already stepping away from her.

Outside of the house, these convention halls were where my father could act like he owned the place. This happened once at the end of a show in Charlotte. I was boxing up the samples we didn't sell when I heard him roar at the first-time exhibitor whose booth was adjacent to ours. She was South Asian, Indian probably, a little younger than Dad, and sold decorative brass and tin urns, which he scowled at whenever buyers gushed over them. "Not classy," he declared. He deemed her line to be a competitor to our porcelain ginger jars and fishbowls and grew agitated whenever buyers wandered over to her booth from ours. Possibly the show organizer drew up the floor plan to create an Oriental wing at one end of the floor. The woman must have done something to annoy Dad, who was already anxious about getting to the loading dock first. Before long, they were going at it, shouting over each other to trade insults, just a couple of feet separating their faces as they jabbed their fingers in the air like puppets.

"Look at your skin," my father said, sneering. "So dark and ugly."

The woman sat back and waited. "I don't understand you," she shot back in perfect Indian English. "You can't even speak English properly."

I froze about twenty feet away. It wouldn't be the last time that I stood on the sidelines when my father needed me. Much to my relief, one of the walkie-talkie junior executives rushed in and separated the two, who even in retreat eyeballed each other like prizefighters. Their fray had shaken me up more than them, these cousins of empire used to threats more terrible than each other. "So dumb," Dad said, shaking his head when he returned to me at the booth. He complained that he had been a part of the show a long time and was going to talk to the owner about moving the woman to the other end of the floor next year.

I envied the other exhibitors at the time, not for myself—I would be gone soon enough—but for Dad, who I wished would take their lead, either the older white glad-handers or the Indian woman, both confident in ways that he wasn't. Dad didn't enjoy himself like they did; he was on edge even with customers. He relaxed only at day's end, when we could share a decent meal at a steak house chain close to the motel. Driving home after a good show, however, he was as carefree as a kid acing his last exam. He could look forward to a few weeks at home, and other than light warehouse work, nothing would arise that my mother couldn't handle herself. I realize now it was because he could count on being around just us, not that we were his proverbial pride and joy—he loved us well enough—but we were a known quantity. We didn't present problems to be solved on the fly, those requiring him to engage with strangers in a language with so much room for error. In the cube van, he stiffened noticeably whenever we neared a state line. "I hate this stupid part," he would say, running his hand over the top of the dash for his daily logbook. At these weigh stations, where we were compelled to halt like all truckers, the state troopers would check our records and either wave us through—even I was relieved—or else squint at our papers before pointing to a spot off to the side for us to park and await further inspection.

*   *   *

There was once a time when my father might have thought about his work differently, not as the means to allow a retreat from the world, but as something that might finally connect him to it, like a language. In the eighties, when I was barely a teenager, he met a businessman named Gary, a husky Oklahoman with doughy skin and a bushy mustache. Gary wore heavy sports coats and Tony Lama boots, which Dad soon adopted as his own dressy footwear. Back then, I knew little about their plan to go into business, only that Dad was excited about it. They traveled to China together, so maybe Gary provided the capital and Dad the connections. Gary was one of the few white men I remember being invited to our house, his broad shoulders and elongated boots making it feel like he was crowding you at the table. The new business was going to be called "The Silk Road," words my parents affixed to the glass door of their showroom with a fancy gold decal and that my father wrote over and over again on cotton bond paper with fat Cross pens. I can still remember Dad researching the actual, historic Silk Road, checking out books from the public library for the first time, engrossed in the glossy images of camels and sand dunes. In time, however, Gary stopped visiting the house, and soon after, I watched my father scrape the decal off the glass a word at a time. My parents never spoke of the soured deal to me, but I still saw Gary at trade shows, with his line of merchandise that was identical to Dad's. He waved at me whenever I walked past his booth, which seemed busier than ours, his buyers happy to linger and shoot the breeze with the friendly cowboy regaling them with tales from around the world.

After the end of "The Silk Road" venture, my father reined it all in when it came to the business, probably blaming himself for thinking that he could ever trust outsiders like family. He solved the problem of Gary by deciding that there wouldn't be others like him. Shih & Co., Inc., kept most of its clients, and business remained steady through those few summers that I tagged along. But it wasn't going to grow beyond what was already imagined for it, not without other people in the picture. Yet as my father hardened his resolve, we kids embraced a more liberal worldview, individualistic and rational, old enough now to look beyond the family to see the future. I didn't know then that I would be the only one of us to leave Texas, but I did know that my prospects didn't align with my father's. I was at the age when people began to ask me—seriously now—what I might like to do for a living. Did I want to take over the family business? An uncle asked me this question in front of my parents, all four of us in the family room. The fathers of my friends weren't gone for what seemed like almost a month at a time. "I want a regular job," I remember saying, more or less. "I want to know how much money I'll make so that I can plan." My uncle, who had earned a business degree at North Texas State University and was a bachelor in his fifties, scoffed at the notion, saying something about my never getting rich that way. "I agree with David," Mom said then, surprising all of us. Dad said nothing.

In its last years, the business contracted at the same rate at which it had expanded after we bought the house. The demand for chinoiserie plateaued, and there were more competitors now, many from mainland China, younger father-son teams I saw squatting and smoking together on the loading docks. The market had opened up by then—anybody could do this now—and people like Gary didn't need to find insiders like my father anymore. Dad stopped traveling to shows and sold the cube van to the uncle who had teased me about being complacent. Dad was seventy-four. I don't think he ever seriously entertained the hope that I would take over for him one day, not even when customers or fellow exhibitors with the shit-eating grins pestered him about when his "number one son" would step up and allow him to retire. Perhaps he wanted to see this first chore to the end himself, saving me from an itinerant life so lonely that you were tempted to search out strangers in the middle of the night on squawky radio frequencies. But he also had to know that the immigrant's kid who shepherds the family concern into the next era is regarded differently from the native son who does the same. Around him is no halo of family stewardship or civic pride, only an air of ancient duty that gives off the tiniest whiff of failure and un-Americanness. The old immigrant lets it go then, this erstwhile dream that what you had built might outlast you in this land.

"You don't know what he's like, because you moved away," Selma told me after Dad retired. "He's different now that he spends all his time in the house." Only at moments of crisis with Dad was I reminded of my infrequent visits by my sisters, who saw his ebbing in real time. As if to fortify the burglar alarm, he now drew an overt line between the house and what lay beyond. It started when he began to skip the First Communions and grade school graduations of the younger grandkids. He commissioned my young niece to design a sign with an icon of a person cleaning up after a dog, which he then staked next to the crape myrtle. When he tired of neighbor kids cutting through the side yard, he anchored two metal posts there, stringing a chain between them like a velvet rope. The sign suspended from it read PRIVATE PROPERTY. KEEP OFF. It resembled the MAKE LOTS OF $$$ signs Teresa used to draw, in design if not optimism. He stopped answering the landline when he was alone, and if he was forced to because he expected to hear from Mom, he would pick up the receiver and say nothing, hanging up after a few seconds if he didn't recognize her voice or one of ours. These changes manifested in stark fashion a year at a time for me, as if revealed in a series of spy plane photographs of foreign installations. It stands to reason that I shouldn't have been surprised by that final piece of intel, the image of his once generous face shrunken and palsied by the clot that had snaked into his brain.

My wife, Robin, and I had "moved away" to Wisconsin. When we decided it was time to buy a house, we toured an old neighborhood dotted with historic homes, some from the nineteenth century that seemed impossibly old to me. The house we bought was a small, prewar Dutch Colonial for sale by the owner on a broad, arterial street once canopied by mature elms. We were one of the earliest to see it the day it went up for sale, aware that if we didn't agree to the asking price, someone else surely would. And though the decision to shake hands on the spot was made with an urgency unknown to me to that point, it was also undaunting and strangely automatic, if only because of how well my wife and I understood where we were in our lives. It was low risk. Only a year before, I'd felt the same way about getting married after a long courtship.

The original owner of the house was a woman who had lived there for fifty years, we heard. She wasn't married, had no children, and moved to a retirement home in the eighties after she sold. Apparently, her neighbors had bristled at the driveway she put in at the front of the house, which spoiled the uninterrupted expanse of lawn that had characterized the street from one end of the block to the other. Rumor was that she once lived with a roommate for many years, a woman, which made me think she too had solved a problem with her house, the one space where she was free to be herself. My father asked if there weren't any new homes in our city to buy, and my mother wanted to know if anyone had died in the house. I didn't mind moving into someone's old house, and I liked its bones—solid plaster walls and copper pipes. It was like the ones I had seen on old black-and-white sitcoms. Coming home was a little like walking into a past I already knew.

As Robin and I grew more comfortable in our new home, my parents seemed to be penned in more by theirs. Home for Christmas one year, I marveled at how efficiently they had migrated their remaining inventory to the house. Without the cube van, they had chauffeured every piece from the shuttered warehouse by themselves, one carload at a time. Their vehicles were now consigned to the driveway, the two-car garage—once such a selling point—rimmed with salvaged plywood shelving and piled high with heavy cardboard crates. At the center was a drill press the size of an NBA point guard and around it a smaller-scale version of the original workshop for wiring porcelain lamps, which they still sold to internet buyers. Teresa's old bedroom was unnavigable, stocked as it was with towers of boxes full of embroidered lace tablecloths and runners. The master bedroom and Selma's room, where Mom had been sleeping by herself for years, were depositories for catalogs and files from the office. My bedroom they had left untouched, I being the only kid who needed a place to stay anymore. "It's like a museum in here," Robin once joked, shaking her head at my dusty old lead miniatures and comic books, undisturbed since my high school days. A couple of parcels for the UPS driver sat neatly stacked by the front door in the same foyer where the family once stood waving goodbye to the cube van. I thought all these changes would sadden my father, remind him of designs left unfinished, but instead he appeared deeply relieved by the consolidation, which must have meant many things to him, but at the moment only that there were fewer debts and obligations to draw him out of the house, repurposed in its dotage like him.

*   *   *

For a time, I believed that it was expected and even natural for white people to move far away from their family once they had the means or even if they didn't. But if my friends and colleagues are any indication, that's not the case at all and never was, the stuff of middle school novels. So many of the otherwise worldly people I've met may have matriculated hours or even states away, but they had enough sense to return like salmon, maybe to the next zip code over, if only to maintain the illusion of homesteading. Their hometowns suited them just fine, they concluded, plenty good for raising the next generation of solid citizens like themselves, who had turned out all right. High school reunions are, at most, day trips. Even now I find myself a little envious of this life

cycle, knowing full well how it also perpetuates a clannish-
ness to be feared and pitied by interlopers like me. At picnics
and barbecues, whenever I observe the locals chatting away
with their parents, at times impatiently, yes, often about the
changes the town is undergoing—premature or quizzical but
almost never bad—I wonder what it must be like to express
yourself so assuredly, not even having to finish sentences
between forkfuls of food, confident that those across from
you know exactly what you mean even if they think you're
a fool, the very trees and sky encircling you a part of the
essential grammar.

My father never said what he thought about the measure of my formal education, whether it was too long and
too much, an extravagance neither of us could afford. He
must have assumed that like anything worth doing, a degree
demanded time and resources. A sacrifice. What made sense
to him here were the professional tracks that turned my
sisters into a CPA and pharmacist. The liberal arts mystified
the arrangement between college and a job, something that
my uncle with the business degree would have said. For a
time, I believed the same. In high school, I didn't get why my
friends combed through catalogs from places like Pomona or
Emerson College when the public flagship was a straight shot
down I-35 and had football. It was like they knew something
I didn't about the future. We had AP courses in common, but

I couldn't fathom the draw of extracurriculars like drama or tennis, whose purpose seemed so indirect. For my parents and me, the logical and proper payoff for studiousness was the letter of acceptance to the flagship's engineering school. Yet after a couple of years, in danger of flunking out, I called them to announce that I was changing my major to English. I'd lost an engineering scholarship in the process, and they would have to pay more to make up for it. "We support you," they said, surprising me with their lack of hesitation and little knowing the extent of their commitment.

Studying English in the eighties was like mainlining whiteness. Like engineering, it had its own developmental sequence: *Beowulf* to Updike. The difference was in their take on past knowledge. In engineering, our network theory professor had paid us a cash bounty for each error we caught in his textbook's byzantine diagrams of circuits. I wasn't looking for such gaps in logic from Jane Austen or Nathaniel Hawthorne, not the way I would eventually teach my own students to do. Our sacred texts were part of a grand tradition, not works in progress subject to a sophomore's blue pencil. In these poems and novels, depth of character had to do with a common quality, I noticed, that of being circumspect, such consideration possible only in the absence of desperation. Except for *Beowulf*, the literature was nothing if not the celebration of options, up to and including suicide. Whole novels were dedicated to assessing the merits of an audacious marriage proposal. Characters were forever weighing this or that decision, men and women alike, it seemed, everyone a Hamlet. I loved it. The more we read, the more we made fun of the stories we liked as children—millionaires hunting humans, children stoning adults—dystopian, it seemed, because all the action left no time for reflection, the characters humanized in direct proportion to the complexity of their motivations.

It was around this time that I started to believe that my parents lacked a certain wisdom in handling their affairs and, in turn, in how they counseled us to deal with ours. As I began to apply to out-of-state graduate schools, my father didn't fully grasp why I needed to leave Texas and the suburbs, their newness a no-brainer upgrade to the blighted urban centers surrounding the trade show convention halls. He made the state's provincial arrogance his own, especially during Cowboys games and beauty pageants. Whenever Miss California made an appearance, he leaped out of his chair and yelled at the big tube television—"What's so beautiful about her?"—only to nod in silent deference when Miss Texas clicked across the stage. The racism he just accepted as a fact of life. He wasn't interested in how graduate school taught me to parse the structure of our Asian lives, and I lost patience struggling to explain in English why it all mattered. Once words like "stereotype" or "economic" crept in, I stopped talking because I sounded like his teacher, which was sad for both of us. When he grew tired and wanted to change the subject, he stabbed his finger on the table and proclaimed, "I tell you, Chinese people will always be second-class citizens in this country," and only much later did I think that he was almost exactly right. He probably believed that I didn't need to go to school so far away and for so long to understand such a simple truth. Yet there he was, loading the cube van with my belongings and pointing it at college towns at the end of alien interstates. Every month I was away, he directed Mom to send a rent check, enough of a Confucian still to respect my teachers and their power to help in ways his allowances could not.

It may be that my father got why I moved away because he had been deep into his thirties when he had done the same. Opportunities arose in places other than where fate had stuck you, he knew, and you trailed them if you were to have any chance of supporting yourself, and not just in the strictest sense. In his bedroom a few days after the funeral, Mom handed over a sheaf of papers that she had pulled from his nightstand drawer full of old forms, appliance manuals, and other printed matter that Dad thought might be important someday. It was his application for British "naturalisation," tendered to the immigration department in Hong Kong, where he had landed with his parents and siblings ahead of the Communists. The eighteen pages are something in between a résumé and a biography, detailing his family line (I wasn't born yet), civic duties, income and net worth, and travel history. On the last page he had to state in his own words why he wanted to become a citizen of the United Kingdom. He listed five reasons. The last one read, "My wife and child are British Subject by birth." He was denied. But then, not even four years later, after I was born and with the implementation of the Hart-Celler Act in full swing, the four of us deplaned in sunny California a year into the new decade. Maybe Dad regarded my graduate school applications in the same light—in this life, some saw fit to spurn you, while others saw enough in you to take a chance, and you repaid that first confidence with a thick, final loyalty of your own.

In the years before his death, whenever our conversations began to trend darkly, Dad, in pain from the reach of his diabetes and almost certainly depressed, would voice his regrets over bringing us to this country. His days now revolved around watching Chinese soap operas piped in through the rooftop satellite dish. "That's Hong Kong," he would say to no one in particular, pointing at gleaming BMWs or skyscrapers on the flat screen, not expecting a response. In the same family room where we'd cheered on

35

those beauty queens, we kids protested, reminding him that his sacrifices had underwritten our lives and liberties, and he would nod, no doubt relieved that we could care for ourselves now. The three of us had our advanced degrees and our own families. This kind of talk had become automatic for me around my parents, saying what was necessary to keep things as they were and nothing that would require new commitments in mind or body. We gave my father back nothing more than the classic immigrant story that was told to us in public school. I think he just wanted his educated children to agree with him for once. Our canned response never seemed to satisfy him at these moments, I felt, as if he yet believed that there should be something more for him than this, a roomful of his own who had been trained to deny him the relief of even the most impotent of fancies.

*   *   *

Language, like blood, can make a family. Even now, a thrill finds its way up and out of me whenever I lecture in a fluent, unaccented English. I watch how the first, familiar tones and cadences ripple the gentlest wave of relief across the faces of my white students. It's not unpleasant, this sensation of having one over on someone you've never met because of what they think they see. It must be like what obscenely attractive people feel when they at last let on that they are, in fact, whip-smart, only without the real power that comes with that combination. It is a rush, nonetheless, to speak like this, addictive in its own way. You seek out those trafficking in the same allusions and tropes, those shared shortcuts of meaning that bring on the knowing nods and snorts that say you belong somewhere, finally. It is as good a reason as any to explain why otherwise ordinary people go on to teach college: the draw of propagating themselves every season like alphas. Your students even begin to sound like you, falling back on to the same crutch phrases, "So you see" or "Does that make sense?" Some will cross their arms and wait out the discussions with their thousand-yard stares. Still, a few will come to you in your office and timidly admit that the world seems different now, both wider and more fraught than the one introduced to them by their well-meaning parents, some of whom, you know, had steeled themselves for the coming apostasy of their own.

I was a year old when I crossed the ocean with my parents and my older sister, an immigrant in name but not in heart. I remember, when I was four or five, sitting at the dinner table and watching my mother uncoil the string from the buttons of the khaki envelope covered in airmail stamps, then tilt the opening toward her palm until a cassette tape dropped into it. She plugged in the National-brand tape recorder, and for the next half hour, she and my father leaned in like radio operators manning a jungle outpost, listening to news from home. In a few days, Mom would make a recording of her own to send back to Hong Kong about our lives in America, perhaps about how they were saving for a down payment on a house in a new neighborhood outside of the city. Selma and I didn't understand much of the Cantonese, but we didn't feel it as a loss or as something that mattered to who we were. Up until my father's death, I'd believed it was a mutual decision between my parents not to teach us kids Chinese so that our Americanization could proceed apace. "It was your father's decision," my mother revealed. "I wanted all of you to learn Chinese, but he said no." I suppose he hoped to spare us the same fear he had speaking English, to smash that barrier to real problem-solving, leaving not a single trace of the old country in our syntax or idioms or the way we said a word like "particularly." It would be a clean break. And it wasn't until that moment when she told me that, and he was already gone, that I realized my going away to school was in fact nothing at all like his own odyssey, only appearing grand to me at the time relative to the meager purview and ambitions of the assimilated and the native.

*   *   *

By most accounts, my father was a bad patient. The stroke had partially paralyzed one side of his body, and all he wanted was to be delivered back to the house. I'd heard that he tried to pull himself out of bed but usually lost his balance and ended up flailing about, too often in the direction of the nurses rushing into the room. Once he grazed one on the backside, and she accused him of trying to hit her. Maybe he was. After that, the staffers put him in restraints when he woke up and his demeanor suggested that there would be further thrashing or just more trouble than they were willing to put up with in what was left of their shift. If my father ever asked for me at these low times, I never heard about it. What he did want and kept asking for, my mother said, was his Rolex Submariner, a souvenir from better days abandoned on his nightstand when the EMTs whisked him from his bedroom. When she retrieved it from the house and strapped it to his wrist, he calmed immediately and even rallied a bit. But eventually the flailing started again, the watch band singing out in time against the bed railing, and Mom took it back because she figured Dad would eventually crack the crystal. "He blamed me for keeping him in the hospital," she told me later. "He asked me to take him home every day. And he kept asking where his shoes were." The day after his heart stopped in the middle of the night and couldn't be revived, Mom recalled, the elderly woman who took over his vacated room could be heard down the hall, plaintively clamoring for her shoes.

According to my sisters, Dad was indifferent or hostile to most of his caregivers, but the one he was least afraid of and even friendly toward was a young nurse, a Vietnamese American woman. I suppose he felt he could be more like himself around her because she reminded him of his daughters. When we were teenagers, my older sister invited her Vietnamese friend Evelyn over for a sleepover, and my father was as warm and generous to her as any television dad. Even now I remember the fine English Evelyn spoke with my father, more articulate than Selma's and like an adult's, and how it surprised me coming from someone who looked like she could be a part of our family. Dad may have liked Evelyn because her manners marked her as part of the first wave of refugees from Saigon, the South Vietnamese state officials and their families who, while fleeing for their lives, still found a way to depart their homeland as we did— by air. But in general, he had no affection for Vietnamese people, seeing these latecomers in much the same way the rest of the country did—as cheap and shoddy versions of himself. He was learning how racism worked in America, where there was no contradiction between accepting your kid's refugee friend on their own terms and turning around to judge a raft of their kind on an entirely different scale.

In time, the nurse lost patience with Dad like the rest of the staff, I heard. Perhaps she mistook his terror for a base meanness that deserved nothing more from her. The hardest thing for some of us children of immigrants and refugees to do is to honor a fear we have never known.

My father's fear at that moment was an immigrant's fear. Not the kind brought on by a white mob or Homeland Security, but a fear of powerlessness all the same. It's the fear of drawing attention to oneself and asking for trouble from the institutions ready to bring it. Barking bank officers and state troopers may have populated my parents' fitful dreams. None of our generation felt that way. Our fear was the kind that spooked the privileged. It was the fear of the unpredictable—the amoeba in the lake water, the texting adolescent at an intersection—that bolt out of the blue to humble you not because of who you were but where. The crucial moment for an immigrant family is when the child ignores or at best humors the fears of their parents, and that's when the balance between them forever tilts. To call a fear irrational is to trust in the status quo, which, for much of our lives, my sisters and I fed like a retirement plan. Everyone ignored my father's demands to go home. Even Mom told him to stay put until he got better. Eventually, Dad grew desperate enough to try his luck on the youngest grandkid in the room with a driver's license, who was eighteen.

Before the rounds of blood thinners and antipsychotics plunged him into a hazy stupor, he and I spoke over

FaceTime. "Mama won't take me home, David," he said. He was propped up in his bed, eyes sunken and half closed, the sight made more pitiful by the loose hospital gown revealing too much of his hollowed chest.

I said he couldn't go home.

"I am *mis-er-a-ble* here," he added, hitting every syllable, the last coherent thought he would ever share with me.

It was too easy to dismiss him. In our family, there was nothing like "the Talk," that grim rite of Black America that nevertheless follows the natural pattern of elders forewarning the young. For Asian Americans like us, the talk takes place in reverse, the assimilated child—impatient and sometimes cruel—telling the parent what they do not know about the world but should: "Listen to your doctors." My father was safer in the hospital than at home, I know and still believe. But what matters to me now is whether, at that dire moment, he was beating back another fear—that of me acting like I knew better, once again. Had I arrived in time, Dad would have asked me to take him back to the house too, and perhaps I would have been the one who disappointed him most by refusing, his lone son like all the rest, telling the old man to stick it out a little longer. It was how I had treated him for almost all my life, from the day I began to excel in school and no longer asked for his help, my distrusts both subtle and overt, second-guessing how he ran his business or his mouth. That I might have been right this last time doesn't help me now if I was also party to his fear.

The difference between my father and me is that, had our roles been reversed, he would have found a way to whisk me out of the room and through the front doors of Texas Health Presbyterian. Back doors, probably. Or he would have tried before getting caught. At the very least, he would have demanded of the doctors and nurses to know why I wasn't getting well, accusing them of incompetence. He would have believed me when I said I was better off at home. That's how he would have shown his love, by delivering me by his own hand to where I had directed, as he used to do. We kids and grandkids knew only how to chirp our love for him like birdsong. It was all the imagination we had. Dad was of another world, not half-ghosts like us. It wasn't complicated. He wouldn't have thrown in with strangers over kin, no matter how educated or esteemed. He would've trusted me, even against his better judgment, for no other reason than who I was to him, just as sons have always been to fathers, divine to despot.

How unalike this country had made us. In some uncharted recess, I must have expected that Dad would once again let me off the hook, fixing a problem before I devoted any energy to it. He would recover somehow, as he did after Gary and after retirement, finding a new way forward without my help. The truth is that I was afraid of what seeing him in the hospital would force me to do, which was decide whether to stay in Texas and help him through an uphill recovery or else an undignified decline. Hoping from a distance was easier. I met problems differently from my father for no better reason than that I could, having grown used to waiting until outcomes were all but certain to pitch in my favor. His solutions trended desperate and final, from quitting an allegiance to a familiar soil to closing his heart to a belated countryman—bold leaps with no easy return. The ultimate one taken in his sleep.

My long education had taught me that words were deeds. It promised that you could build a life out of language, one I now didn't want to quit. At some point I began to believe that each word I spoke or read or heard was a solution in its own right. I was like a scribing Puritan or a senator in filibuster. In me, my father got not what he needed but what he had blessed: an American son with the ability to tell him no in a thousand ways when it mattered the most.

Maybe intimacy for my father and me can happen only after death, when, no longer parted by a rift between grammars, the child can at last confess the truth of the land to the parent. The child would start by saying that this country turned him against his parents just by sending him to school. He learned to look upon the parent falsely, as the powerful did. Then he would say how he learned to do the same to himself. At the end, he would say he did it all because of a latter-day folk tale they both knew, which was ever the promise of a better life. I would speak those words now. I would chant the words with incense smoldering between my fingers. I would write them on gold paper and set them on fire, kiting them to the sky and beyond for the dead of other clans to envy, which I think must be the purest Chinese American offering to an ancestor.

*   *   *

After the funeral, my mother said that she was glad to have me back at the house, if only because my father was due to return to it a week after his death. If all went well, the Ox-Head and Horse-Face deities would escort his spirit through the house and then on to judgment in the afterlife. It was a homecoming but also the final one. Our first responsibility was to prepare the food. That night, Mom steamed a batch of pork dumplings, setting them next to the incense pot on the old student desk she used as a shrine. My sisters dropped off candy bars, soda, and a tube of summer sausage, snacks-to-go reminiscent of Dad's days in the cube van. I added a Styrofoam take-out carton of andouille sausage and red beans and rice from Pappadeaux, the only restaurant food Dad liked at the end. I blew up his old passport photo and put it in a gold frame next to the offerings. My flight home left the next day, and this was my last night in my old bedroom for a while. Mom admitted that she was a little scared, unsure if Dad still blamed her for keeping him in the hospital. "Don't stay up late like you usually do," she said. "You're supposed to be in bed when they come." For reasons she didn't explain, the trio would arrive at precisely eleven o'clock. I decided to turn out the lights ten minutes before and try to fall asleep. But I couldn't, slowly beginning to feel a little anxious myself there in the dark. I was wondering whether ten minutes had already passed when a wailing siren screamed out from somewhere inside the house. It lasted several seconds, long enough for me to turn on the light and check the time.

As I got ready to leave for the airport the next morning, I asked Mom if she had heard the siren too. I assumed it had originated from the old burglar alarm, which occasionally tripped by mistake. It had woken her up as well. The noise had come from her flip phone, she said, which was automatically set to broadcast Amber alerts.

At eleven o'clock the night before, out in the dark but somewhere close by, a child had gone missing, and a parent, maybe two, were wide-awake and retracing the arc of their day, pleading with the observant, despite the late hour, to please do something.

CHAPTER 2
THE BOOK OF GENESIS

When I was younger, given the construct of my desire, I must have assumed, at some level, that my children would be mixed race, half Chinese and half white. However, for most of that period, I would not have populated whatever eugenic fantasy was playing out in my head with words like "mixed race" or "biracial" or "multiracial," probably because I had not seen or heard them used in that way often enough to register. Not having the words was part of the problem of being assimilated. Beyond the responsibility to secure the financial means to keep them safe, I did not consider whether there would be an ethical dimension to the decision to have mixed-race children in the United States. How would they be treated by monoracial people—Asians and white people, mostly— and how would they treat themselves as a result? These questions are long-standing enough to be cliché, revived each generation with different principals and vocabulary.

Yet while the questions may remain the same, the meanings of the groups in question are only as stable as their relationship to each other—and to other racial groups—which is why the questions continue to be worth asking. To the extent that his mother and I lose the interest or will to answer them, whatever doubts about identity that I deferred or buried while growing up in segregated residential and educational spaces will return tenfold for our son, I imagine, because of the meaning that others will make of his body and name, yes, but also because of the choices that I have made to put him in that same position.

Not long after we were married, Robin decided to stop using birth control pills in favor of the Depo shot, which required an injection once every few months. This solution lasted for about a year before the progestin hormone kicked up enough side effects to convince her to quit the course. Ultimately, we decided to stop using birth control altogether. We weren't actively trying to become parents—no hip-raising or cycle-calculating routines—because we didn't feel as though our lives would be empty without children. By this point we were both professionals in our early thirties and, in our minds, prepared for parenthood, not so much reckless as confident in the way that education, resources, and a sense of belonging will make a person. Even so, our preparation didn't include a serious discussion of what it would mean, either for us or for our children, that they would be mixed race. When Robin continued to have a period for several months after going off birth control, we wrote it off as the lingering effects of the progestin, which we had heard could take a while to leave the system. But with every passing month, I silently began to adjust to the prospect that it was probably going to be just the two of us for the rest of our lives, which to me was plenty, a lifestyle common in academia. We had been off contraceptives for several years when, one morning, I rolled over in bed to see Robin floating in from the bathroom and holding a little stick. "Look at this!" she said. She had been silently adjusting too, but to the responsibility of a life we had long assumed to be out of reach. Later, we did the math and concluded that like so many other children of color born that year, Jacob had been conceived on the night of Obama's first inauguration. He arrived not even two weeks before I turned forty, the age when a person begins to wonder as much about their past as their future.

*   *   *

If there is one thing that white nationalists and liberal progressives agree on about the future of the United States, it is the inevitability of its browning. They simply disagree about the meaning of such a future. In 2015, the Census Bureau issued a report projecting that by 2044, more than half of all Americans would belong to a minority group, all but non-Hispanic white people, the so-called majority-minority narrative. Political pundits and scientists alike have credited this narrative for fueling the rise of the white nationalist movement and for stoking a general fear of social change that helped to put Donald Trump in the White House the next year. According to the Census Bureau, between 2010 and 2020, those reporting multiple races increased from 2.9 percent of the population to 10.2 percent, a jump largely attributed to improved instrument design and processing but significant nonetheless. Given the small size of the Asian population relative to that of Black and Latino populations, the "white and Asian" population punched above its weight, increasing by 1.1 million people, almost as many as the "white and Black or African American" population. Mixed-race Americans factor significantly into the political tensions anticipating a majority-minority future, making the rhetorical struggle over the meaning of their identity vital to our understanding of the state of American racism in general. As forward-facing as the narrative may look, it is an old story.

Literary scholars generally acknowledge that the first Asian North American fiction writer was a mixed-race woman who was born Edith Eaton but later changed her name to Sui Sin Far. Far, whose father was British and mother was Chinese, published her best-known piece, "Leaves from the Mental Portfolio of an Eurasian," in 1909. The autobiographical essay is a series of vignettes that mostly dramatize the moments when acquaintances of Far discover that she is not white. Although Far describes a life of privation owing to the discrimination she faces as a single "Eurasian" woman, she takes solace in the possibility that the future may be brighter. "Only when the whole world becomes as one family will human beings be able to see clearly and hear distinctly," she writes. "I believe that some day a great part of the world will be Eurasian. I cheer myself with the thought that I am but a pioneer. A pioneer should glory in suffering." As early as the first decade of the twentieth century, progressive periodicals entered the conversation about whether mixed-race people had a demographic destiny as the solution to racism. In its original form in the *Independent*, Far's essay is topped with a portrait photograph of the author, whose eyes make contact with those of the reader and seem to invite a closer look at her face.

Beginning in the early 1990s, the heyday of the multiculturalism movement, the meaning of mixed-race identity in the United States within popular culture became increasingly defined by the physical body, especially by phenotypical facial features. In 1993, *Time* magazine published a special issue entitled "The New Face of America: How Immigrants

Are Shaping the World's First Multicultural Society." The cover featured a computer-generated image of a woman's face comprised "from a mix of several races." In 2001, the artist Kip Fulbeck began the Hapa Project, a multimedia exhibition based on photographs of mixed-race people of Asian and Pacific Islander ancestry. Fulbeck followed up the Hapa Project with his *hapa.me* exhibition in 2018, which included photographs of his subjects fifteen years later. ("Hapa" is a Hawaiian word, originating from the English word "half," which can refer to part-Asian people, although native Hawaiians and others sometimes see this broad usage as an act of cultural appropriation.) In 2013, *National Geographic* magazine published a feature entitled "The Changing Face of America" that included a series of photographic portraits by Martin Schoeller intended to showcase the phenotypic diversity of mixed-race people across the country. This feature inspired a Mic think piece by Zak Cheney-Rice entitled "*National Geographic* Determined What Americans Will Look Like in 2050, and It's Beautiful." In response, Jia Tolentino, writing for the Hairpin, refutes the assumption behind celebrating a comely multiracial future: "Look at how beautiful it is to see everything diluted that we used to hate."

Any liberal gesture at the transcendent beauty of the multiracial body is premised upon the white supremacist logic of eugenics, namely the absence of beauty in the non-white monoracial body. How else, Tolentino wonders, is a woman perceived as multiracial judged to be beautiful, for example, compared with a woman perceived as Black? Praise for mixed-race phenotype is either praise for whiteness or scorn for Blackness, often both. My father made no secret of his preference for Jacob's looks among those of all his grand-children. But Jacob unwittingly baited him and so many others, inheriting his mother's eyes and hair and complexion, a kind of genetic trifecta in this country. To be sure, Jacob was prized in our family as the only boy of his generation with our last name, but his looks sealed the deal on his crowning. "Good-looking boy," my father chanted. "Handsome boy." Dad carried on about Jacob's features, his peachy skin and blond baby hair especially, patting the boy on his back as he spoke. I was more sickly looking at that age, my hair coming in patchy and standing straight up. Jacob could grow up to be whatever he wanted, Dad told him—"A senator!"—a blessing that he never bestowed or could bestow upon me. Even my father saw my son auguring a rosier future, one that, if he didn't know to call "post-racial," he hoped would at least make room for the coming of our blood.

My son's body was the one signal of his identity that I had something to do with but over which I had no control. Because I was looking for something else, I may have been the only one in the birthing room surprised by his round eyes and not-black hair, an epiphany I would later joke about with friends and even strangers. "Where's my Chinese baby?" I spouted, calling upon our common knowledge of Mendelian genetics, what must be our true national curriculum. The truth was that I too was proud of his looks, the way they would always shade more white than Asian, like the student body at an Ivy League school. I was both old and aware enough not to gush in front of others, especially my friends and colleagues of color, because you don't do that if you are like me and your partner is white. Our silence has nothing to do with the mock humility of new parents amid gushing friends. It is about how our fight with white supremacy checks even our delight in our own, an instinct as natural as fear. The nature of my pride at that time spoke to my own unfulfilled claims of belonging, in the unhealthy way of sports dads and pageant mothers.

My pride was contingent on where we chose to reside, not only our city but our neighborhood, where Jacob would live among and go to school mostly with children who looked like him. It was one thing for Robin and me to choose Eau Claire, Wisconsin, as our home and another to choose it for our son. The house we had owned for eight years proved large enough for the three of us, and we didn't consider moving to a more diverse neighborhood in town or even ninety miles away to Minneapolis–St. Paul, as some of my colleagues at the university had done. Jacob saw my sisters and their kids only once a year when we made it back to Texas for the holidays. Robin took the lead in arranging play-dates with children of color—mixed-race kids themselves, mostly—and I presumed that other white parents who valued diversity liked having Jacob around partly for that reason too. I must have told myself that I had done all I could do to secure for my son a healthy sense of himself and of others, but the reality was that he might come to normalize the lack of diversity in his life, and I didn't want to see that as a problem, at least not one that would justify disrupting a routine that had become comfortable and affirming for me.

As Jacob grew older, I found better things about him to be proud of, valuing his behavior over his biology. His face waxed softer and rounder, and his hair turned a rich copper. His heterochromia, which colored one eye brown and the other green and would have certainly enticed *National Geographic* to our home, began to fade, and I guessed he would be a brown-eyed man like his father. People no longer commented on his attractiveness—unseemly past a certain age, surely—and instead some would say to me, perhaps after studying him for a moment too long, "He's really beginning to look like you."

*   *   *

After Jacob was born, my mother gave me a sheet of printer paper with his Chinese name written on it. My father, who had chosen the name, must have asked her to do it because her handwriting was better. On the right side of the sheet, she had used a black Sharpie to stack the three characters in a single column. On the left side, she had written the characters in yellow highlighter and numbered each individual stroke (thirty-three total) in ballpoint pen. I still can't copy them elegantly, not even hunched like a scrivener, something to do with pressure. The first two characters are also part of my own name, our last name and the first half of the given name. The third, the other half of the given name, is Jacob's own and means "virtue." I could tell, when he got older, that he didn't like how the word sounded in Cantonese, a little like "duck," which is one of your funnier animals in this culture thanks to cartoons. While she was at it, Mom made a sheet for my name too, which I still have to consult every now and again.

There was never any question between Robin and me that our son would go by his Christian name and not his Chinese name, partly because that was what I had done. As a kid, I believed that my Hong Kong birth certificate had given me permission. "David" is written above the two characters of my Chinese name, Da Wei, in the column "Name, if any." It took my grandfather a couple of days to come up with my name after he sized me up in person, but the recordkeepers still had plenty of time to pencil it in before the birth certificate was issued. Every given name in a Chinese family line is unique. On the other hand, ultrasound technology and family tradition left little doubt about what we would name our child. "Jacob" was the name of my father-in-law, the fifth in his own family to have it, and the stars were aligning in a way that would make our son his only grandchild. I've always liked the name "Jacob," and I don't think that I ever objected to the choice or even humbly asked to discuss other options with Robin. I didn't invite my father to choose a name for our son until after the matter was settled. According to Social Security card application data, "Jacob" was the second-most popular boy's name in both Wisconsin and Texas that year. The most popular boy's name in Texas was "José." Topping the charts in Wisconsin was "Ethan."

In a 2008 article published in the *Sociological Review*, Rosalind Edwards and Chamion Caballero reported that the naming decisions for mixed-race children in the UK correlated with a tension within interracial partnerships between what are called "pro-race" and "post-race" positions. The former is a race-conscious position that acknowledges either the salience of Black identity in society or else the need for a separate mixed-race category. The latter position is closer to the futurist vision of Sui Sin Far and Zak Cheney-Rice, which supposes that hybridity and mixed-race identity will somehow destabilize the logic of racial classification and deconstruct the social hierarchies dependent on it. Edwards and Caballero found that the two positions were not as discrete as they might appear, in that "traditional boundaries, categories and customs are being transcended at the same time as they retain salience and effect." They concluded that the "complex collective affinity aspects of naming children . . . is likely not to be evident in research that relies simply on birth name registration records. . . . [A] full understanding of naming practices . . . can only be gained through also asking parents about the process behind their choice of their children's names." This is what the scholar and activist Sharon Chang did to research her 2015 book, *Raising Mixed Race: Multiracial Asian Children in a Post-Racial World.* In talking to dozens of Asian-white couples in Washington state, Chang found that what they named their children created significant tension between the parents and within their larger families. "My parents were worried that we were going to name [our son] something crazy," said one interviewee. "To them 'crazy' would be some Japanese name that they never heard. . . . My mom . . . really gravitates towards names that are really more American; easy, Pottery-Barn-ish. You know . . . like Jacob, or Ethan, or Aidan." Robin and I didn't have that problem.

In 2019, the comedian Hasan Minhaj tweeted out a segment from *The Ellen DeGeneres Show* in which he steadfastly corrects the host DeGeneres on the pronunciation of his name. Minhaj went on to address the viral moment on his own show, *Patriot Act*. He decided to make a point, he explains, because he saw his parents in the audience cringe when DeGeneres mispronounced his name. On the ride home from the interview, Minhaj was criticized by his father for wasting airtime schooling DeGeneres. The big difference between their generations, Minhaj says, is that "they're always trying to survive. And I mean survival is the thing, so just go by whatever she calls you. And that's cool. I think when Dad . . . came in '82, he survived for us. But I'm trying to live. I mean, I'm trying to like, 'Yo, Muhammad Ali, say my name. Like, say it.'" Over the past twenty years, on official forms and on social media, my Hmong students have increasingly eschewed not only their American names but the alphabet with which to spell them. These names, like "Pajyeeb" and "Vajfwm," spelled in the Romanized Popular Alphabet, demand attention and humility from non-Hmong people, scarce resources among some professors. One student admitted that she suffered her professor mangling her name for the entire semester because it eventually became too awkward to correct him. In 2020, Matthew Hubbard, a white professor at Laney College, sent an email to his Vietnamese American student Phuc Bui Diem Nguyen. "Could you Anglicize your name. Phuc Bui sounds like an insult in English," he wrote. When the student threatened to file a complaint, Hubbard doubled down: "I understand you are offended, but you need to understand your name is an offensive sound in my language. I repeat my request."

The statute of limitations for Asians accommodating the ethnocentric sanctimony and glib detachment of authority figures like Hubbard and DeGeneres, Minhaj implies, is over. In fact, he continues, in this regard, Asians should be more like Black Americans, who know something about naming in this country. Muhammad Ali renounced his birth name, his "slave name" "Clay," for the name given to him by the Nation of Islam leader Elijah Muhammad. I knew that by selecting "Jacob" for our son, we would not be asking non-Chinese speakers—including me—to do a little extra when they encountered him, to stress themselves and their syllables beyond their custom. What I didn't know then was that consenting to the name turned on a pair of unexamined assumptions on my part. The first was that our son was not truly Chinese, not like my father and me, so I must have regarded the name that my father gave to him as a token, like the ones indigenous elders in the movies bestow upon interlopers with hearts of gold. The other was that, unlike Minhaj's parents and my own, in the main, I was able to live in this country and not just survive. I did not need to look to the future because the present had been acceptable, if not hospitable. My last name eventually outlasted the juvenile squints and sneers directed at it, and it proved no barrier to Robin accepting it as her own. Researchers concurred that interracial parents took seriously how a name might expose their mixed-race children to discrimination. What parents don't want their children to belong to the world they are born into? The difference between Minhaj's parents and me is that I knew the cost of such inclusion. "What belongs to you, but other people use it more than you?" So goes the children's riddle.

Jacob's middle name is my own first name, "David." When I told a Jewish friend my son's full name, he smiled at me and cried, "Mazel tov!" When Jacob was older and asked about the meaning of his name, I had some homework to do. The story of Jacob is one of the more confusing in the Bible. My son was troubled by the part where the biblical Jacob cheats his older brother, Esau, out of his inheritance, deceiving his father in the process, and then goes on to spend a lifetime in exile. To stall, I began by saying that Isaac and Rebekah didn't think they could have children either.

Also that Jacob was the favorite of his mother, who labored to safeguard for him the stingy blessings of his father. I didn't say that the most remarkable trait that he and his namesake shared at their birth was the fairness of their skin. But the more I researched, the more I grew to love the story of the biblical Jacob, more so than that of the biblical David. I liked that the biblical Jacob was not a perfect man. He told lies to get what he wanted, but he was in turn deceived by others. It seems to me that he was a self-conscious person for his whole life. He was used to seeing himself through the eyes of others, even the blind ones of his father. It wasn't always for the right reasons. He had to struggle to do the right thing; it did not come easy to him. Then, finally, he dreamed of a ladder that bridged heaven and earth and was told that the country of his father and his grandfather belonged to him too. Jacob chose to fight a powerful being for that country and won. After this, Jacob no longer went by his old name, his new identity fit for a nation.

*   *   *

Our son has been counted in two different census periods now, and both times we have marked two boxes for him under the "race" question, "white" and "Chinese." Once, I overheard Jacob—he was eight or nine—telling my father-in-law that he was "half Chinese, half white," an identity that Jacob had heard me ascribe to him many times before. His grandfather corrected him: "No, you are half Chinese, half Caucasian." Although this annoyed me, I accepted that his need for euphemism could have been worse. Maybe my father-in-law thought that "Caucasian" sounded more objective or scientific than white (even though he must have seen "white" on census forms too). Or more polite. He may have associated "white" with the creed of white supremacists and decided that he wanted none of that. I'm just glad that he left the "Chinese" part intact and didn't steer the conversation in a more dubious, color-blind direction. After all, he could have said something like "You're not half of anything—you're a whole human being!" or "I'll tell you who you are—you're *Jacob*!"

When I joked about not seeing a Chinese baby at Jacob's birth, I was invoking, albeit ironically, a racist idea known as the rule of hypodescent, colloquially referred to as the "one-drop rule." For mixed-race people, the rule of hypodescent equated their social status with that of the parent or ancestor with the lesser status. In this way, it created a single, inferior caste, "Black," to oppose to "white," but in so doing it also created a community. Scholars trace the invention of hypodescent to the Chesapeake region of colonial America where, in 1662, a half century after English settlement, the Virginia General Assembly openly questioned whether the children of an "Englishman" and a "negro woman" should be slave or free. It took less than thirty years for the same body to conclude that laws were needed to "prevent . . . abominable mixture and spurious issue" between "negroes, mulattoes, and Indians" with "English, or other white women." Soon enough, however, the rule of hypodescent began to drive the economic engine of Black chattel slavery, especially after 1807, when Congress abolished the importation of enslaved people from foreign locations. Thomas Jefferson had long endorsed ending the foreign slave trade, even though his children by Sally Hemings were enslaved and freed only after his death.

It wasn't until 1910 that the census included a data item specifically for race (called "color or race"). The first census, in 1790, directly placed people into the categories of "free white" boys, men, and women; "all other free persons"; and "slaves." A "free colored persons" category arrived in 1820, and 1850 saw the addition of the "mulatto" category, which lasted until 1920 (excepting the 1900 census). "Chinese" and "Indian" were added in 1870, the same year that the "mulatto" category included "quadroons, octoroons and all persons having any perceptible trace of African blood." Separate categories for "quadroon" and "octoroon" were added in 1890, testifying to the increasingly granular obsession with hypodescent. "Japanese" also appeared that year.

In 1930, "Mexican" was added (only to be removed in 1940, when Mexicans were white again). By 1930, however, the "mulatto," "quadroon," and "octoroon" categories, along with the "Black" category, were collapsed into the "Negro" category, where any amount of Black ancestry would land you. The census has always regulated access to rights and responsibilities by policing the edges of whiteness, races coming and going, either when they start to seem like a social problem to the ruling order or when they stop seeming like one.

Prior to the civil rights acts of the 1960s, mixed-race people categorized as non-white circumvented social barriers—to citizenship, to marriage, etc.—by passing as white. Openly claiming a mixed-race or multiracial identity without penalty was possible only after the end of de jure segregation rendered moot the juridical function of hypodescent. Yet, in a racialized society, hypodescent still informs one's de facto status, and mixed-race people today still choose to pass for white. I wanted Jacob from an early age to know that he was half Chinese, because I did not want him to go through life passing as white, meaning that I did not want him to leverage, consciously or not, white privilege for his benefit and to the detriment of those who could not pass or those who could but refused to. And if Jacob thought that he was all Chinese, well, that would be fine too. But in an era without a state-enforced rule of hypodescent to turn Jacob Chinese, it was and still is unclear to me which community he will be left with.

None of this is to say that enforced hypodescent dispelled the tensions stirred by colorism within non-white communities. In "Leaves from the Mental Portfolio of an Eurasian," Sui Sin Far refuses to turn up her nose at the "Chinamen" wearing work blouses and with queues wrapped around their necks. Yet the "Americanized Chinamen actually laugh in my face when I tell them that I am of their race," she adds. It's possible that my son will face a similar reception from other Asian Americans who do not identify as mixed race themselves. The researchers Jacqueline Chen, Nour Kteily, and Arnold Ho wondered whether mixed-race Asians would be seen as more Asian than white by monoracial Asians, the way that mixed-race Black Americans are usually seen as more Black than white by monoracial Black Americans. "Asian Americans in our sample," Chen writes, "tended to see Asian-White people as wanting to be White, more loyal to White people, and more White than Asian." These responses were more common among Asian Americans who believed that the racial discrimination against them was "severe." This may mean that Jacob will find it harder to connect with Southeast Asian Americans like my Hmong students, especially the men, who have been profiled in ways that locate them, racially, closer to Blackness than to whiteness. At twelve, Jacob has Hmong friends in middle school, but I fear that their camaraderie will strain if and when they notice how he is treated differently—better—by their white peers and teachers.

When my son is older, I will continue to say that he is half Chinese, half white, but I will also tell him that the matter of his race is often beyond his control. At any given moment, he will be whatever race whiteness needs him to be. He will be white; Chinese; or half Chinese, half white. It does not have to be a curse if you know what is happening to you and can survive. Something similar happened to me. When increasing diversity aggrieves a ruling order, such as the members of the Virginia General Assembly, our country predictably needs its subjects to be monoracial, even as its most optimistic say "multiracial" or "biracial" or "mixed race" or "half Chinese, half white"—all the words I didn't have as a boy—without a second thought. Those words have been bought for us by the abasement of generations one-dropped into the backs of buses and by the anxiety of the brothers, sisters, and cousins whose daily passing at their workplaces supported a family. Those words deserve more than how they have been deployed—to center race instead of racism in public life.

* * *

In her 2014 article "The Current State of Multiracial Discourse," published in the *Journal of Critical Mixed Race Studies*, Molly Littlewood McKibben lays out the "critical difference between post–civil rights black pride and late-century multiracial affirmation." The former "employed traditional racial categorization for political unity, whereas the multiracial movement challenges the same racial categories in and of themselves." McKibben critiques two major positions within the multiracial movement. The first is that multiracial identity should be considered an identity group unto itself, with the commonality of being "mixed" in the abstract standing in for a shared phenotype or social history as the basis for group identity. The second position is that multiracial identity should allow for the shedding of racial group affiliation altogether with the goal of claiming identity as an "individual." Both positions are in contrast with the way I counseled Jacob to think about his race, which, looking back, was one of the good decisions I had made about ordering his sense of place in our mazy world.

When he was a freshman in college, Ryan Graham asked his mother for counsel on what race to call himself. Graham, whose father is Black, had been invited to pledge a Black fraternity at the University of Florida but had identified as multiracial his whole life. When he was a boy, he and his mother, Susan Graham, who identifies as white, founded an organization called Project RACE (Reclassify All Children Equally), dedicated to getting government agencies and private companies to recognize a "multiracial" category on their official forms so that people like Ryan were not forced to select one race or another. According to Susan in a 2017 op-ed column she wrote for the *Orlando Sentinel*, Ryan was "the youngest person to ever testify before a congressional subcommittee in Washington." Early on, the column abruptly shifts to the topic of affirmative action. "We've never used affirmative action," Susan told her son, whom the university had classified as white. "Anything you've gotten hasn't been based on race." The column concludes like a holiday letter, updating readers on Ryan's latest accomplishments: he passed on the Black fraternity, graduated college, is "gainfully employed," continues to identify as multiracial, and rejects affirmative action for himself. "His life is based on his character and not on the color of his skin. Isn't this the way it should be?" Susan asks.

Susan Graham's story about her son outlines the major positions within the multiracial movement and reveals how they might strategically intersect to imperil current state policy benefiting those who identify monoracially, such as Black, Latino, and Native American people. The position that multiracial people should have their own racial category seems progressive in that it doesn't deny race as part of identity, but it also doesn't offer a logical basis for group cohesion (such as a history of state-based discrimination). In a 2015 survey conducted by the Pew Research Center, only 17 percent of mixed-race adults said that they had a lot in common with people who are a different mix of races than they are. My nephew, who is half Chinese, half white, told me that he was once asked if he were Mexican or Italian. There is very little that mixed-race people can take for granted as a group commonality, and, in the end, the impatience or anger that may arise from being asked "What are you?" is not enough. For one, my nephew was neither impatient nor angry. Also, monoracial people such as actual Mexicans and Italians are also asked "What are you?" Two of Jacob's good friends from elementary school are mixed race, each with a Black parent and a white parent. I suspect that his friends have never been asked what they are. The question of "What are you?" has more to do with the maintenance of white identity than with an interest in multiracial identity.

The aim of Project RACE may not end with updated census and SAT forms. In 1997, following his victory at that year's Masters Tournament, the golfer Tiger Woods told Oprah Winfrey that growing up, he called himself "Cablinasian" because of his Caucasian, Black, American Indian, and Asian heritage. (At the tournament, fellow golfer Fuzzy

Zoeller told reporters to tell Woods not to "serve fried chicken . . . or collard greens" at the following year's Champions Dinner.) Given the idiosyncrasy of "Cablinasian" and its meaninglessness as a social category, Woods's comment marks a key individualist turn within popular multiracial discourse. In arguing that multiracial people should be treated as individuals rather than as belonging to a parent's monoracial group, Project RACE finesses the discourse of race consciousness to advance a color-blind policy agenda seeking to delegitimate group-based resource claims such as affirmative action. Predictably, Susan Graham co-opts language from Martin Luther King's "I Have a Dream" speech to push this rhetorical strategy. Her son is the word made flesh. And because their natural talent and work ethic ensure their success in a seemingly meritocratic field like professional sports, figures like Woods become even more powerful symbols of a post-racial future: the multiracial person who is, before anything else, an individual.

Yet when multiracial athletes make personal decisions as individuals that challenge the function of hypodescent— the maintenance of a white supremacist state—public opinion swiftly descends to chastise them. The world-class tennis star Naomi Osaka, whose mother is from Japan and father is from Haiti, identifies as Asian and Black. Born in Japan and raised in the United States, Osaka chose to represent

Japan at the 2020 Summer Olympics in Tokyo, surrendering her American citizenship in the process. The backlash from the decision included critics telling her that her "Black card is revoked," Osaka revealed in the 2021 Netflix documentary about her. "African American isn't the only Black, you know?" she returned. In 2022, the freestyle skier Eileen Gu found herself mired in a similar controversy. Gu was born in the United States and raised by her Chinese mother; her father, rarely mentioned in Gu's media coverage, has been described only as an "American." Gu may have given up her US citizenship to compete for China at the 2022 Winter Olympics in Beijing. Despite a history of Olympic athletes switching national allegiances, she endured the opprobrium of a company of critics, Fox News's Tucker Carlson and Will Cain calling her "ungrateful" and accusing her of "betraying her country." Gu was expected to be a Chinese American who knew her place. "Part of the Eileen Gu perplexity," explains the sociologist Russell Jeung, "is that the West is seen as superior and the East is seen as inferior. So why would she want to represent China?" When novel expressions of mixed-race identity challenge the premise and function of hypodescent, albeit with the help of powerful state actors like Japan and China in the cases of Osaka and Gu, they reveal the unspoken and long-held racial allegiances of American nationalism.

Far from anticipating the future, mixed-race identity has served to remind us of the past and its potential to invade the present, to the frustration of those who would seek to move on. Jacob was not yet one when his parents' optimism about Obama's election began fading away. The radical prospect of mixed-race identity is neither the elimination of extant racial categories nor the addition of a "multiracial" category to go next to them. It is the disruption of the logic that feeds them. After all, the census already had added a "multiracial" category in 1850 under a different name, and what the word "mulatto" accomplished was to create more non-white people still Black enough for re-enslavement by the Fugitive Slave Act passed the same year. Whiteness has never had difficulty with making room below itself. "I have no nationality and am not anxious to claim any," Sui Sin Far writes. "Individuality is more than nationality." Unlike Susan Graham, Far looks forward to the advent of individual identity and an end to racial categories because she understood that the invention of race was coeval with the invention of its meanings. To the extent that mixed-race Asian Americans portend a post-racial future in the white imagination, Black Americans must continue to signify a violent, indelible past of enslavement and segregation. Following her Grand Slam victory at the 2020 US Open, Naomi Osaka responded to a question about the seven masks she wore throughout the tournament, each one bearing the name of a Black American killed by police violence. "What was the message you wanted to send, Naomi?" ESPN's Tom Rinaldi asked at center court. "Um, well, what was the message that you got?" Osaka replied. She seemed to say to him, "You go first."

*   *   *

Ever since Jacob was an infant, I liked holding him in my arms in public, even knowing what that might mean for us. It's not often that you see an Asian man cradling a white-presenting baby in this country, and I warned Robin that someone might think that I was kidnapping him. If it happened, I told myself that I would say that I adopted Jacob from England, where baby boys are unwanted and abandoned. Another joke at my son's expense, one my mother hated. ("Don't kid around about adopting him," she said. "Jacob's yours.") Part of me wanted a confrontation like that, however, if only to prove to at least one person that I wasn't who they thought I was. But it never happened. Jacob and I weren't as familiar a pair as a white woman and her Asian baby but also not a sight worth calling the police over. All the same, I did get reported once.

One weekend, when Jacob was a toddler, our family took a short trip from our home in western Wisconsin across the Minnesota border to the city of Apple Valley and the Minnesota Zoo, a favorite destination. It was there that a little girl snitched on me. She must have been about five or six, old enough to be by herself without a parent hovering by her side. Her skin was tan and her hair as black as mine used to be. Her eyes resembled my own, rounder than those of most Asians, but she was clearly mixed race like Jacob. If our child had been a girl, I would have expected her to look the same way in time. Robin was off somewhere on her own, and it was just Jacob and me strolling outside of the swine barn. The little girl stood there staring daggers at us. I smiled but got nothing back. Maybe she was lost and was turning to a familiar face for help, I thought. But she grew increasingly upset, not letting up for what seemed like forever. Then, to my alarm, she raised her skinny arm and pointed at us. She turned to a white woman I hadn't noticed nearby.

"Mommy, why is Daddy holding that little boy?" she said.

The woman clasped the little girl's raised hand in her own and gently lowered it to her side, then drew the girl against her own body. "I'm sorry," she said, shaking her head. "You look a little bit like my husband." She gestured at an Asian man standing about ten yards away. He was probably Chinese or Korean, younger than I was but of similar build, and wore glasses and short, cropped hair like mine. Our clothes were completely different. I was glad that he didn't notice me looking at him.

After they left, I ran through the possible explanations for the little girl's fit. Perhaps she was big for her age or had a disability that impaired her vision or social skills. The sun could have been in her eyes. Maybe such cases of mistaken identity were developmental in nature, perfectly normal. At age five, I myself might have raced up to some Asian stranger at a playground, expecting them to scoop me up and take me home. I mentioned the incident to my Japanese colleague. The next time we ran into each other, my colleague said, "I asked my mom if I ever did that, and she said no. Children in Japan don't do that." Eventually I concluded that the little girl did not have many Asian people in her life beyond her own, which was how I grew up and how Jacob could too. The families at the Minnesota Zoo, I noticed, were mostly white or white and Asian, less diverse than those across town at the Como Park Zoo in St. Paul, where admission was free. Apple Valley itself is not as homogenous as its tonier counterparts ringing the Twin Cities, but it is still predominantly white, its demographics in line with those inside its zoo on any given day. Maybe the little girl's confusion resulted from nothing more complicated than segregation, the usual suspect behind the sense that people of color look the same. This was probably it, I told myself, growing angry at the ways that racism had clouded the vision of the little mixed-race girl, even when it was trained on those most dear to her. Perhaps I also worried about how Jacob, when he got to her age, would regard me, replaceable because of my race, nothing like his mother.

I long for a lesson from my instant with the little girl, something good to keep from that brief spark of her notice. The writer Jeff Yang once tweeted, "#BeingAsian means looking for The Nod . . . and half the time, letting your eyes slide away embarrassed when it doesn't come." I wonder why blood did not build a family for us as broadly as it did for Black Americans. Of course, we were never part of a criminal conspiracy like slavery, whose viability depended on the fiction of race. Passing may have been easier for us, the penalties for discovery milder; Sui Sin Far outs Eurasians—her sisters, probably—passing as Spanish or Mexican as my nephew could have (one sister, Winnifred Eaton, passed as a Japanese writer). But part of the answer must be our inability or reluctance to empathize with other Asians based on the wrongs that they have known or might know, as Yang says. The scar of "severe" discrimination fails as the acid test of a true Asian American identity, especially if it is to include mixed-race people. We ought to be able to see ourselves in others for no better reason than that we ought to know the truth of what racism has done and can do—even if its worst harms have missed us. And not because a distant pain may in time come to visit us too but because it probably won't. My father came to this country so that his children would meet with less struggle, and now I will have to ask my own child to claim it with the hope that he will not have to glory in suffering too. One day, I met a little girl who saw someone she loved slipping away from her and into the crowd, and she called out with the words that she had, in shock and then relief that she had got there just in time.

CHAPTER 3
IT'S NOT FAIR

I n 1982, outside of Detroit, Ronald Ebens and his step-son, Michael Nitz, stalked a Chinese American man named Vincent Chin through the city of Highland Park, where the headquarters of Chrysler Corporation was located. The three had met at the Fancy Pants Club, a topless bar where the twenty-seven-year-old Chin was celebrating his bachelor party with three close friends. His wedding was a week away. According to witnesses, Ebens and Chin began loudly arguing with each other. "It's because of you little motherfuckers that we're out of work," shouted Ebens, who was in fact employed as a foreman at Chrysler at the time. Ebens had assumed that Chin was Japanese, or close enough for his needs. The men brawled inside the bar before taking their fight to the parking lot, where Nitz produced a Jackie Robinson Louisville Slugger from the trunk of his car. Chin fled. Ebens and Nitz hired an accomplice and cruised through the neighborhood before spotting

Chin and his friend Jimmy Choi outside of a McDonald's. While Nitz held Chin in a bear hug, Ebens swung the bat at Chin's knees, ribs, and skull, beating the helpless man so badly that a responding EMT reported seeing his brains on the pavement. Ebens and Nitz were sentenced to probation and a fine on a plea-bargained manslaughter charge. The efforts of community activists led to federal charges against them for violating the civil rights of Chin because of his race. While Nitz was acquitted, Ebens was convicted, only to have the verdict overturned on appeal. The new federal trial was moved out of Detroit to a neutral site free from publicity about the case, and it was there that Ebens too was acquitted.

Vincent Chin had been dead for over ten years by the time I heard of him. I was twenty-three and a graduate student in creative writing at the University of Oregon. The director of the program was the Japanese American poet Garrett Hongo, whose plans to build a diverse writing cohort involved me, I was surprised to learn. No part of my application's writing sample—two or three short stories—indicated that I was interested in writing about being Asian American, or that I might be the victim of racism because of it, least of all at the hands of a system that seemed to be working for me. Garrett invited the poets Li-Young Lee and David Mura into the program as visiting professors and assembled a group of Asian American MFA students that included Chang-rae Lee, who was drafting what would become his first novel, *Native Speaker*. It was about a Korean American man who learns, a little too late in his life, what a sense of belonging in this country has cost him. Chang-rae was only a few years older than I was, but the shining prose he shared in workshop left most of us unable to add anything except our congratulations. In workshop, I appreciated his generous comments on my own stories, which usually complimented my craft or technique. Maybe it was because we had become friends over the first year of the program, but near the end of it, he opened up a bit more about the subject of my writing. "David," he began one day, "can I ask why your stories are all about white people?"

It was at the writing program in Eugene, when I was well into my twenties, that I began to think about myself as an Asian American. It wasn't so much the writing but the reading. I discovered Asian American writers I had never heard of before, including Japanese Americans published during World War II and in its aftermath, pioneers such as Hisaye Yamamoto, Wakako Yamauchi, Monica Sone, and John Okada, who were also interested in what might happen to you if you were considered Japanese in this country. It was possible even to study being Asian American in graduate school, I learned, an identity whose meaning, like any

81

other, depended on who or what had the power to make it stick. In my last year at Oregon, I was accepted into the doctoral program in English at the University of Michigan. I had never been to Michigan and knew nothing about the state. But the university awarded me a good fellowship, partly for being Asian American, and I would have the opportunity to work with the scholar Stephen Sumida, whose research focused on recovering an Asian American literary tradition of resistance. My application had included my first attempt at Asian American literary criticism. "Congratulations," Chang-rae said when I told him the news. "Ann Arbor?" He paused, nodding. "Vincent Chin, man."

I learned that to call yourself "Asian American" on purpose meant knowing about Vincent Chin. Chang-rae had given me the briefest and most remedial of lessons. The term was supposed to connect the three of us in a way I didn't yet apprehend. In 1968, Yuji Ichioka and Emma Gee, students at the University of California, Berkeley, coined the term when they founded the Asian American Political Alliance to unite Chinese, Japanese, and Filipino students in a fight for ethnic studies on their campus. But it was the notoriety of Chin's brutal murder that brought the term into the mainstream. Like any other idea, it needed a story to bring it to life. Vincent Chin was Chinese American, but Ebens and Nitz needed him to be Japanese to blame him for their anger at Toyota and Datsun, which must have seemed like impudent upstarts too. "Asian American" is an all-American story. To be Asian in this country and learn about Vincent Chin was to find out that you were related to someone you'd never met before. Our kinship didn't trace back to Asia, to any custom or language we might be assumed to share. It could be born only here. What Vincent Chin and I had in common as Asian Americans was our vulnerability in America. We were vulnerable to being made into people we were not and were therefore vulnerable to the sanctimony and to the violence that too often followed. As the legal scholar Frank Wu put it, "Before the Vincent Chin case, it's fair to say there weren't Asian Americans." Vincent Chin, thanks to those fighting for justice in his name, invented the Asian American.

*　*　*

I had grown up in north Texas, one of those ostensibly neutral sites that promised Ronald Ebens a fair trial. American Citizens for Justice (ACJ), the civil rights organization calling for the federal case against him, had no presence in my hometown. As a kid, I didn't notice anything that led me to believe that Japanese people could be a special target of discrimination. The one exception, I remember now, was a local commercial for a domestic car dealership on late-night

TV. An actor dressed in green army fatigues, perhaps the owner himself, chased after and lobbed grenades at a terrified and retreating man—Japanese, I suppose—to prove that the dealership wasn't going to be undersold. The commercial may have amused me at the time. There weren't many Asians in my neighborhood besides us. The Wongs, a retired couple two houses over, occasionally brought us fuzzy gourds from their backyard garden. A boy my age with dark skin lived a few blocks down. Sanjay wore white undershirts like regular clothes and propelled a skateboard down our street with his bare feet. His parents must have been immigrants like us, but nobody considered Indians to be Asians like Chinese back then. Sanjay and I played together a lot during grade school, but by the time we got to junior high, neither of us made much of an effort to maintain the relationship. The year Vincent Chin was killed, I was in eighth grade and trying my best not to think about myself as Chinese, so it helped to have friends who were white, which Sanjay wasn't.

My best friend, Brad, lived in a fancier subdivision of custom homes about a half mile away. His mother was a teacher at another school and carried herself like a patrician, once correcting my pronunciation of "etiquette" with obvious relish. Later, I learned that her father was wealthy, which explained why Brad always received expensive birthday and Christmas gifts from him—home computers and clothes by Le Coq Sportif and other designer brands none of us had ever heard of. I never met the man, but Brad told me that he had made a lot of money during World War II as a member of the Flying Tigers. I didn't know who the Flying Tigers were, but it seemed important for Brad's mother to tell me that they were heroic American fliers who protected the Chinese people from the "Japs." I liked that I wasn't a Jap. I spent the night over at Brad's often, and we would stay up late watching the Playboy Channel once he unscrambled the cable box. In the seventh grade, Brad was the first one to know that a girl I had asked to "go" with me had said yes over the phone. "I can't believe it," Brad said. "Amy is dating a chink!"

Brad and I weren't as popular as we wanted to be. This may have had something to do with how much we loved computers. We tried to program a video game together on our Texas Instruments models to sell out of the back of hobby magazines. Being more athletic would have been a better plan. At our junior high school, I opted for the regular PE class instead of organized athletics. Out on the football field one day, I must have been joking around too loudly with a classmate while our bullet-headed teacher in his short shorts was still talking. Our teacher went silent and glared at me. He was white and obviously a former college athlete. "This time is mine, Mr. Shih," he began. "When you go home and play with your *Wang* computers, that is your time, but until then, please keep your mouth shut." Some kids laughed. I don't remember whether I apologized—I probably did—but I did know that what he had said to me went beyond what I had expected or deserved. It was 1982, the same year that Vincent Chin died. Chin was good at computers too. He was a terminal operator and draftsman at Efficient Engineering Co. in Oak Park, Michigan, which did design work for automotive companies like GM. He wasn't a Japanese autoworker but an American citizen who was part of the domestic auto industry. It wouldn't have mattered to Ronald Ebens, just as it wouldn't have mattered to my teacher that Wang Laboratories was an American outfit.

The day on the football field was unusual for me. I earned perfect attendance awards and was mostly quiet in class. Something about me had set off our PE teacher, who didn't reproach whomever I was talking to. It was easy for him to turn my inattention into insolence. I was small for my age, wore glasses, and might have looked especially vulnerable in my own navy short shorts with SHIH spelled out in yellow iron-on transfers. It bothered my teacher that I wasn't taking him seriously, which may have led him to infer that I wasn't taking his job or even physical education seriously. Maybe he thought I was talking about him in Chinese. Maybe I was already on probation in his eyes for not going out for basketball or track like other boys my age. Maybe he thought saying "Wang" was funny, because he counted on everyone knowing that an Asian penis meant "bad at sports." Maybe he was a Vietnam vet who didn't care about the differences among Asians the way the Flying Tigers did. In any event, I was a bad student at school that day, a turn of events that could have happened only in PE. I didn't bother to tell my parents, who didn't have the words to explain how my teacher was trying to shame me. I knew I wasn't in the wrong. But I didn't know to say that my teacher was being racist.

*　　*　　*

Vincent Chin's legal team had the same dilemma. The Wayne State University constitutional law professor Robert Sedler advised the ACJ lawyers to drop their federal case. Existing civil rights laws were meant to protect African Americans, he said, not Asian Americans, who were considered white. Ronald Ebens became the first person prosecuted for violating the civil rights of an Asian American based on their race. Because of the prosecution's erroneous handling of evidence, he was granted a second federal trial upon appeal, this time in Cincinnati, where local news cameras weren't trained on domestic autoworkers sledgehammering Japanese imports. The activist and author Helen Zia, the past president of the

ACJ, found that only nineteen of the 180 people in the jury pool "had ever had a 'casual contact' with an Asian American." Ebens's fate hinged on whether jurors believed that "It's because of you little motherfuckers that we're out of work" meant that Chin was targeted because of his race. Almost five years after his death, a jury of ten white people and two Black people didn't. My PE teacher would have agreed. Even I didn't know what words like "go home and play with your Wang computers" were doing, even though they stung. The pain was in the gap between who you thought you were and who others thought you were.

By all accounts, Chin was not who Ebens expected him to be. He had been naturalized as a citizen when he was ten years old. Family photos showed Chin to be a happy and confident young man—posing beside a muscle car or open-shirted in swim trunks or sporting shades and a gold chain, grinning widely. "Vincent fit in very well," his friend Gary Koivu recalled. "He learned the ways of America, and he didn't seem to be handicapped by the fact that he was Chinese." Chin loved to read and was often found with a book in his hands. He was also athletic, running track and playing football as a teenager. What had bothered Ebens so much about the young Chinese man that night at the Fancy Pants Club? Was it that he had insulted Ebens's favorite dancer, which was like insulting Ebens himself?

"Boy, you don't know a good thing when you see one," Ebens jeered.

"I'm not a boy," Chin replied.

"Hey, you little motherfucker!" Ebens shouted at him.

Chin walked to the other side of the stage and shoved the older man, who shoved back. Maybe Ebens couldn't abide that Chin, according to Angela "Starlene" Rudolph, the favorite dancer, was "the only one standing" after the fight inside the club. Ebens and Nitz were "on the floor" after Chin had "busted them up by himself," said Rudolph. Could it have been that Ebens didn't like how, in the parking lot, Chin had dared him to fight some more? Whatever the reason, Ebens's taunts reminded me of all the older white men in my life who expected us Asian boys to know our places on their turf, to shut up and take notes.

Ebens has consistently maintained that the trial's publicity set him up for a life full of hardship. In 1983, he was fired from his job as a foreman at Chrysler's Warren plant. Following his acquittal in 1987, he avoided the press because he didn't trust reporters to treat him fairly. Months later, he settled a civil suit that required him to pay, in monthly installments, $1.5 million to Chin's estate. On the heels of that settlement, two years before the debut of his documentary *Roger & Me*, Michael Moore talked Ebens into an interview for the *Detroit Free Press*. Moore was surprised; Ebens was unaccompanied by his lawyers and still involved in a pair of pending lawsuits. In a remarkable interview, Moore methodically leads Ebens toward his code red moment: an assertion that *he* was the one victimized by the trial. He wasn't the real racist and couldn't have berated Chin over the plight of the auto industry, he claims, because, at a topless bar, he was preoccupied. Yet Ebens can't help but volunteer his opinion of Japan. "Shame on us for just letting them beat us," he says. "We give them the technology and then let them beat us with it." The Asians "all stick together," he adds. "Why don't white people stick together? Huh? Not 'til we're a minority?"

Before Michael Moore, the filmmakers Christine Choy and Renee Tajima-Peña sat in the same living room with Ebens. In an interview for the Academy Award–nominated documentary *Who Killed Vincent Chin?*, Ebens rehearsed the responses he would give to Moore. The civil suit had not yet been settled. Yet Ebens seemed to believe that what he said would not incriminate but exonerate him. "I'm not aware of any plight [of Asian Americans]," Ebens admits. "I know very few Asians, and the ones that I do know have been very nice people. In fact, my daughter used to help an Asian kid at school." How did this white man, pilloried by activists in the streets and in the press as a racist, endeavor to clear his name after years of silence? Ebens's psychology is not complicated.

The Japanese, once an inferior understudy, had upstaged Detroit. Something was wrong, and a jovial Vincent Chin with money to burn in the Fancy Pants Club symbolized it. In 1987, things finally seemed to be returning to normal for Ebens following his acquittal on federal charges. He hinted that Lily Chin, Vincent's mother, would not collect a fraction of what he was ordered to pay her (she didn't). He was hopeful that he would win his lawsuit against Chrysler for wrongful termination (he didn't). And the next generation of Ebenses was explaining to Asians about the way the world worked, not the other way around.

* * *

Ebens wasn't the first to make the Chinese into the Japanese. For a long time, words like "Asiatic" enabled people like him. In 1906, the Asiatic Exclusion League lobbied the San Francisco School Board into segregating ninety-three Japanese students into a Chinese school, an international crisis requiring none other than President Theodore Roosevelt to step in and deescalate. The "Asiatic Barred Zone" sprang from the 1917 Immigration Act, and in 1924, the Johnson-Reed Act closed the door to all Asian immigration, ensuring decades of more conflation. After Pearl Harbor, Chinese in the United States worked hard not to be made into Japanese. A December 1941 issue of *Life* magazine featured an article entitled "How to Tell Japs from the Chinese." A photo depicted Joe Chiang, a Chinese American reporter, who had pinned a handwritten sign onto his lapel: CHINESE REPORTER NOT JAPANESE PLEASE. In 1943, the dust jacket of *Father and Glorious Descendant*, one of the first Chinese American autobiographies, announced that its author, Pardee Lowe, "enlisted in the U.S. Army shortly after delivering the manuscript of this book." Subtitled "A Story of Chinese Life in America," the bestseller was also released in a special Armed Services edition. That same year, the United States dignified its ally China by rescinding the 1882 Chinese Exclusion Act. A boy could be forgiven if he thought that World War II would end the willful ignorance once and for all.

In the seventies and eighties, people from other Asian groups joined the crowd to muddle the picture even more. They were refugees displaced by the Vietnam War and its aftermath. At my high school in Texas, there weren't many Japanese Americans, so I was rarely made into one. But every year brought more Cambodians and especially Vietnamese. When I was a freshman, early into the semester, a chubby white kid who sat next to me in class leaned in toward my desk. "Hey," he said. "Where are you from?" I was used to this question, but the askers were usually older and more polite with their language. I said I was Chinese. "Good," he replied, which relieved me. "I wanted to make sure you weren't Viet Cong. If you were Viet Cong, we would have a problem." I had never heard "Viet Cong" before, but I was glad that I wasn't one of those either.

"What if he was Vietnamese?" said another student, who had been listening to us. He was another white kid, taller than the chubby kid and me, and even now I remember how his voice was unusually deep for a teenager. He had shoulder-length dark hair and a rail-thin build that made him look like Iggy Pop. We didn't know each other, and before then I assumed that we had nothing in common. He was a "stoner," one of the freaks we dismissed because we thought they did drugs. Stoners wore trench coats and hung out in the smoking area with other stoners just like Judd Nelson in *The Breakfast Club*. He was looking right at the chubby kid, who I could tell was intimidated.

"I just don't like Viet Cong, is all," the chubby kid muttered.

The stoner wouldn't let it go. "No, I mean, why would you not like him if he's never done anything to you?" He rarely spoke in class, so I hadn't realized how articulate he was.

"It's cool," the chubby kid said, desperate to drop the subject.

A white person had never stood up for me like that. I didn't thank the stoner because it didn't occur to me to do so. Maybe he read the newspaper like adults did and had heard of Vincent Chin. I was ready to move on, content to have established that I wasn't Viet Cong. After all, what did I have in common with the Cambodians and Vietnamese at our school, strangers whom everyone, it seemed—even teachers—called "boat people" without thinking twice? I didn't need to pin a homemade sign to my clothes, I figured, because it was obvious that I wouldn't be mistaken for them. But the truth was that I would be, no matter what I did, a reality I thought seriously about and resented. I wasn't like my father in his disdain for them, but I didn't go out of my way to be friendly. Neither did I become friends with the stoner. But I did feel happy for him when I learned that the school had recognized him for his poetry, which he was invited to read at an assembly before his graduation. All I remember about his poem was that it was long and impassioned and quite pointed about the hypocrisy of American forefathers, the stoner methodically chanting off the names of people whom I hadn't heard of but now instantly disliked.

When we talk about Vincent Chin, we should say that what made him an Asian American was that he knew what Ronald Ebens saw in him that night in the Fancy Pants Club. When Ebens made him Japanese, Chin said only, "I'm not Japanese," and not, "You are mistaken, sir." Chin wasn't like any of the yellow minstrels I saw on television, like Charlie Chan. Chin declined to say, "You must have me confused with someone else." Nor did he declare, "I am a proud American of Chinese descent." The precision of this rude white man's xenophobia wasn't his problem. Chin knew exactly where Ebens was going when he said, "It's because of you little motherfuckers that we're out of work," and that Ebens didn't care whether he was from Japan or not. Chin was in no mood to give a geography lesson. He stood up for himself without throwing other Asians under the bus. He didn't have to wear a button or write a memoir. He simply knew that the meaning of his face to Ebens wouldn't change no matter what Asian language came out of it. Chin understood what race was. He knew how it was different from being Chinese around his mother and fiancée, different from ethnicity, how in this country your skin bespoke not your origins but your place in a hierarchy. According to his friend Jimmy Choi, who comforted him as he lay dying in the street, the last words Chin ever spoke were "It's not fair."

*   *   *

Lily Chin was the face of the movement for justice for her son. In 1961, she and her husband, who had served in the US Army during World War II, adopted a six-year-old boy from a Chinese orphanage. David Bing Hing Chin died only six months before his son, Vincent. For millions of Americans reading the papers or watching her on *The Phil Donahue Show*, Lily Chin was a study in bravery and determination. Many "remember her as the grieving mother," Helen Zia recalls, "but to know her—she was a strong, outspoken woman." In pained, halting English, Lily spoke out at rallies and community gatherings asking for help. Yet Ebens's acquittal robbed her of a desire to stay in the United States. Months after the last trial, she moved back to Guangzhou. Ebens had paid only $3,000 of the civil settlement. In 2001, Lily returned to the United States for cancer treatment but died the next year. I wonder how much it mattered to her that in standing up for what was right, she had birthed an idea promising to turn strangers into cousins. "We have been drawn together by death," Jesse Jackson told a San Francisco crowd in 1984, moments after embracing Lily. "An unplanned family reunion." Lily never planned to be the catalyst of the Asian American movement. I think she just wanted her son to come home.

Asian American identity came too late for my parents as well. Despite my career, they never called themselves "Asian Americans." They said "Chinese" or else "Oriental" if they had to refer to themselves as part of a group, no different from so many other immigrants of their generation. Reporters in the eighties, doing their best to capture the scope of the nascent movement behind Vincent Chin, also called him an "Oriental." Ebens said it on the witness stand. "Oriental" was the word Americans used if they were being polite and either didn't know where we were from or didn't care. They used it when they had to talk about a bunch of us, usually too many, who seemed to speak different languages. Yet the word didn't have the power to foster any kinship between my parents and Chin. It wasn't designed for that. It was a word from above, a management tool. "Oriental" was familiar to my parents because people in Hong Kong said it too, China being east of Europe before it was east of the United States. Once he settled in Hong Kong, my father's father, my ah yeh, named his import-export business Oriental Products & Trading Co. Ah yeh manufactured piece goods like silk brocades and sold them around the world. His best customer was German. My father had worked his way up the ladder of the family business to the title of "import supervisor" before he began to think about moving west with his own family.

Especially later in life, my father didn't see himself having much in common with other Asians. His first inclination wasn't to look for similarities, only for what might set him apart from more recent immigrants. With every year that passed, finding affinity was harder because new people kept coming. The one Asian group he seemed to respect

was the Japanese, which I suspected because of the care he
lavished upon his Nikon camera and Sony TVs and because
he never called them "Japs." It wasn't until I was twenty-one
years old that he told me he'd lived under occupation. I
thought he was Manchu because his grade school was in
Manchuria. The oldest photo we have of him is as a boy of
seven or eight, unsmiling among his siblings in front of their
house there, his head shaved nearly bald. Because of what
I was learning about race and identity in graduate school at
Oregon, I must have made a passing reference to being half
Manchu. "You're not Manchu," he replied. "Ah yeh only sent
me to school there. You're Han, just like me." I was calmed
by that news, I remember, the eugenic notion of purity and
an association with the dominant group still mattering to
me despite my political awakening. I became more ashamed
by that realization after my father died, when my mother
told me that while he was away at school, my grandfather
made a living by trading textiles and sundries with the Japanese in occupied Shandong. I hadn't expected my father's
family to be resisters, but it was quite possible that they
were collaborators. "Your grandfather hid bags of Japanese
paper money under the beds," she said. "He burned it and
all of his sales records when the Japanese surrendered."

I never found out why aah yeh sent my father to school
in Manchuria, or Manchukuo, as they probably had to call

it, the name of the puppet state created by imperial Japan. Maybe he thought that his first-born son would get a better education there and would be safer in a pan-Asian future ruled by imperial Japan. Less likely, he felt shame for trading with the invaders and didn't want his son to witness it. As a schoolboy, my father took field trips into what is now North Korea by crossing the Yalu River Bridge, later renamed the Sino-Korean Friendship Bridge. He regularly consorted with Han, Manchurian, Japanese, and Korean people, all part of the "Greater East Asia Co-Prosperity Sphere," the only term clunkier than the "Asian American Political Alliance." I hope that my father was still enough of a boy in those days to make friends across ethnic lines, however blurred by imperialism. In my most generous moments, I might say that my grandfather was flexible in his sense of who his people were. Every time I visit my parents' house, I see his portrait in a gilded frame directly above the sand-filled urn lanced with joss sticks. At the end of the day, we were his only true people.

The only Asian friend of my father's I remember was another immigrant from Shandong. Tom Yung had headed to Taiwan after the Revolution in 1949 while my father's family fled for Hong Kong, both parties perhaps escaping Communist reprisals. They met completely by chance at my parents' merchandise showroom in Dallas. His name was Tien-Man, but we kids called him Uncle Tom. In the seventies, finding a countryman so close must have been heady for my father, especially so far from either coast. Uncle Tom and his wife lived in Louisiana, where they ran a gift shop, but he was also a professor of economics at Grambling State University. Back then, I didn't know that Grambling was an HBCU, but now I'm heartened by the story of it taking a chance on an Asian immigrant so long ago and of that immigrant making his home there for the rest of his career. In 1976, the year all of us except Teresa became citizens, my family went so far as to visit the Yungs at their house, a commitment to sociability on the part of my father that strikes me as amazing now. I was six years old. The bond he felt with Uncle Tom probably went beyond their hometown, extending into their present as Asian Americans—Chinese and Taiwanese—living in the South. The Yungs had a daughter the same age as Teresa, the only one of us who was born here. My mother remembers how the girls, both two years old and potty training at the same time, sat side by side on portable plastic toilets. We drove from Dallas to Ruston, famous for its Peach Festival. I barely remember that trip, but I like to think about the symbolism of our families gorging ourselves on the most Chinese of fruits in the shadow of a historic Black university. The visits dwindled over the years as my father began his slow retreat into himself. Maybe he saw Uncle Tom as what he might have been if the war and the Communist Revolution hadn't interrupted his studies. Or maybe his view of Uncle Tom became tinged with the same suspicion and even disdain that white Americans reserved for Asian newcomers, their erstwhile allies from Southeast Asia.

A word better than "Oriental" wouldn't have made a difference in my father's life, not if he couldn't witness its ability to improve it. Yet I was going away to school for another five years to try to learn that word. Lily Chin had learned it over the worst five years of her life. In addition to the University of Michigan, I had applied to other graduate schools, including the University of Texas, my alma mater. The miles between our home and the campus in Austin were nothing to my father, a world traveler since boyhood. "A letter came today from UT," he told me over the phone. I was on spring break from Oregon with my girlfriend's family and had all my mail forwarded to the house in Texas.

I asked him to open it.

There was a pause. "Rejected," he said.

I hadn't yet heard from the other schools, but I wasn't going to live in Texas again. My father asked me if I was sure I wanted to do this. I could always join the family business, he offered. At the time, I didn't know how to explain to him what I wanted to do for a living. All I knew was that it had to do with teaching others what it meant for people like us to come to this country, or to be born in it, and then have the way that you look stand in the way of your success and happiness and even survival. The only thing I knew to say was "I think I want to become a professor, Daddy."

"Of course, of course," he said. "Your uncle Tom is a professor," he reminded me.

The word I left home to learn was so big that it was actually two: "Asian American." They were a mouthful—too many syllables—kind of like what they stood for. But they were words of my choosing, not like "Asiatic" or "Oriental." I had to work to get others to say them too. I was always correcting friends who didn't want us to have a race or were stingy and asked me to pick "Asian" or "American" but not both. In the nineties, telling the people you grew up with that you were in school for Asian American studies was like speaking gibberish. Even now you can't really count on the people you're with to use the term "Asian American" in reference to you or to what's happening in the world, because they've never had to. In 2021, Leading Asian Americans to Unite for Change (LAAUNCH), an Asian American advocacy organization, reported that 42 percent of respondents couldn't name a single prominent Asian American (Jackie Chan, who isn't Asian American, and Bruce Lee were next at 11 and 9 percent, respectively, among those giving it a shot). Being an Asian American in this way meant struggle, a commitment that didn't really end, a little like being a resister. My father would have thought that was crazy, to choose to struggle indefinitely, especially when the lure of not having to do so, at least economically, was why he left home himself. What I learned and wish I could have told him is that we had to keep fighting because so much was out of our control. I couldn't ever stop learning to be an Asian American because what it meant didn't stay put. Who we were to others in this country depended on what was happening elsewhere in the world. Pearl Harbor. My Lai. South Central LA.

In 1993, the first year of my doctoral program, Vincent Chin became a priority for me. I was researching a paper that tried to connect the development of Asian American literature in the eighties to an awareness of Vincent Chin. I wrote to the ACJ for information. It had been over a decade since Chin's death. Opening the thick manila envelope was like a matriculation. My name was handwritten on the mailing label along with that of the sender—Nati Jenks, the ACJ's longtime executive director. Inside were photocopies of newspaper clippings along with the ACJ's 1983 yearbook and an official statement on the Chin case. In a section entitled "What Does the ACJ Believe In?" the organization explained that "Asian Americans, along with many other groups of people, have historically been given less than equal treatment by the American judicial and governmental system. Only through cooperative efforts with all people will society progress and be a better place for all citizens." The ACJ's list of supporters included Chinese, Japanese, Filipino, Taiwanese, and Korean groups. The movement had a purpose. It was also diverse and, like any other declaration of identity, came with risks. One chose to be an Asian American despite the visibility and threat of more discrimination. In Michigan, people still remembered Vincent Chin, and we spoke his name on campus, but it also seemed like his memory was fading elsewhere. Around the nation, the community that had rallied around him was already changing by the time I had discovered it.

In the nineties, new immigrants complicated the coalition galvanized by Vincent Chin. Like me, many of them had never heard of him and didn't know that we were supposed to stick together. By and by, they had their own historic events to deal with, such as the day when a fifteen-year-old Black girl named Latasha Harlins walked into Empire Liquor Market in LA. The shopkeeper, a Korean American woman named Soon Ja Du, thought Harlins was trying to steal a bottle of orange juice. After a scuffle, Du shot Harlins in the back of the head as the girl was walking away. Harlins had the money for the juice in her hand.

Like Ronald Ebens, Du was convicted of manslaughter and sentenced to probation and a fine. Du seemed to have less in common with Chin than his killer.

But Asian immigrants would soon be swept into an identity movement surpassing that from Chin's era. The violence in LA triggered by the acquittal of the LAPD officers who beat Rodney King hit Korean-owned businesses especially hard; Empire Liquor Market was burned to the ground. Although media coverage tended to frame the conflict in Black and yellow, the racial demographics of the rioters were diverse too, and Koreans in LA resented how they were left to guard their lives and property on their own without police, who were largely dispatched to affluent white neighborhoods. Photographed on rooftops armed with pistols and rifles, Korean men on the lookout for Black looters became folk heroes for white supremacy, but they understood that the system was working against them too. Angela Oh, the best-known spokesperson for the Korean American community at the time, stated plainly, "Korean America was born in 1992." These Korean immigrants became Asian Americans right around the time that I did.

When I contacted Renee Tajima-Peña in 2020, it had been twenty-seven years since I had written to the ACJ, exactly as long as Vincent Chin was alive. I said that I taught *Who Killed Vincent Chin?* almost every year. She told me that there was more to the story. In *Asian Americans*, her latest documentary, the segment on Korean Americans in LA followed the one on Chin on purpose. Chin and Latasha Harlins had something in common that people were missing. Tajima-Peña admitted she was troubled by the way that some remembered Chin. To them, he was a symbol of grievance and injustice, his meaning "fossilized" in the eighties. She meant that Asian Americans shouldn't see the injustices against us in isolation. To be Asian American was to be a part of something bigger across time. It wasn't only about bringing monsters like Ronald Ebens to justice. Rodney King was also beaten by white men with sticks who walked free. Being Asian American had to do with naming whatever protected Ebens and Soon Ja Du and the LAPD and all the buildings that were not on fire in South Central LA in 1992.

During our writing workshops at Oregon, Chang-rae shared chapters of *Native Speaker*, but not the one in which a Korean American councilman named John Kwang attempts to calm a restive crowd in Queens after the deaths of a Black American named Saranda Harlans and a Korean American named Charles Kim. "Know that what we have in common, the sadness and pain and injustice," Kwang intones, "will always be stronger than our differences." Reading the chapter then would have made a difference to me. What I had to go away to learn seems so simple now: what made you Asian in this country wasn't your body or what was inside of it but what was outside of it. Asian-ness wasn't revealed in the fold of your eyelids or the sheen of your hair. It wasn't fixed. Being Asian was more like being a quick-change artist, turning Japanese, Chinese, Vietnamese, Korean, and Hmong at the drop of a hat—whatever the audience needed us to be to keep their own story going. "How does it feel to be a problem?" W. E. B. Du Bois asks himself and other Black Americans in *The Souls of Black Folk*. Less than a hundred years later, in *The Karma of Brown Folk*, Vijay Prashad asks South Asians, the would-be model minority, "How does it feel to be a solution?" In the future, I might not even need to be Asian anymore. Before the shooting of Michael Brown in Ferguson, Missouri, I would joke around with my students by saying that in twenty years I would be white like most of them. There was nothing natural about being white or being Asian. We were made that way not by some higher power but by cartographers. There was nothing natural about being Asian American either. We invented Asian American identity because we needed it. And I needed to learn that being made into an Asian problem or an Asian solution was less about me than about white and Black and the ugly alchemy of profit and pain keeping them in their place.

* * *

Racism isn't always a matter of life and death for Asians. The guilty aren't all like Ronald Ebens, who needed to make Chinese into Japanese to prove that he was an American. They're not usually like James Nichols either, who shot and stabbed Cha Vang in the Wisconsin woods and covered his body with leaves because he had to make all Hmong hunters into Chai Vang, who had killed six white hunters in the state a few years before. They need not resemble Adam Purinton, who decided to make the Indian engineer Srinivas Kuchibhotla into a terrorist before blowing him away in a Kansas bar. Racism isn't always born of hate, although what we read or watch or share about such crimes may lead us to believe it is. If it comes, the hate comes second. The sense of authority, entitlement, or belonging comes first, making more of us responsible. The term "hate crime" did not enter the vernacular until the nineties, well after Vincent Chin's death, but it has too easily become the standard for the presence of racism. In 2021, Robert Aaron Long murdered eight people, including six Asian women, whom he made responsible for his own desires. When the Cherokee County Sheriff's Office explained that the Atlanta spa shootings were the end of "a really bad day" for Long, it made the killer into a victim. Understandably, the fight to call his act a hate crime was also a fight to acknowledge that anti-Asian racism exists. But turning people into things does not have to be hateful to be racist.

Making Asian Americans into a problem or a solution can take less dangerous, if not less delusional, forms. If only their occurrences were less predictable. It might occur when your colleague at work can't remember your name and instead calls you by another, again and again. It is almost certainly the name of another Asian in their life, maybe the only other one. Maybe that other you is a foreigner, because people we do and don't know make us into foreigners every day without putting us in the hospital or morgue. More than once I've been introduced as a specialist in Asian literature instead of Asian American literature, and someone has been disappointed they can't talk to me about Haruki Murakami or Yukio Mishima, whom I really ought to read, I am told. Once, my in-laws hosted a party for Rotary Club scholarship students studying abroad. My wife had spent a year in Germany as a junior in high school. I was approached by a young man hoping to study in Japan. "Where are you from?" he asked hopefully. When I said, "Dallas," he blinked and backed away slowly. It wasn't the first time someone had made me into a foreigner, but it was the first time a person did it who wanted to be made into a foreigner too, at least for a year. Why didn't he know better? The kid was no Ronald Ebens and probably never would come close. But they were still bound together by how they made an Asian into another one only to be wrong and still walk away thinking that the fault had somehow been ours. The problem belonged to the kid, or to the who and the what in his life, not to me. Again, his racism wasn't a matter of life and death. Eventually a word was invented to describe these little aggressions, a word that was for the aggressor's benefit more than mine because it doesn't make anyone say "racist." I didn't need a new word to know why these people from my life felt entitled to make me into something they needed me to be. Each one of them helped me to practice being a better Asian American, like a sparring partner.

The making can go in another direction too, one more reason it is hard to stay Asian American. It would be simpler if I were turned into only Japs, Viet Cong, al-Qaeda, and Kim Jong-un. But I can be made white too, which also speaks to the needs of the maker. In middle and high school, my white friends told me that they didn't think about me as Chinese. In time I caught on that I didn't perplex them with my English like the students who were refugees. When I was a young professor, on my way to class, I often ran into a colleague from the math department, usually in the stairwell. He was much older, a bit frail, a full professor, whose name I could never remember until I finally broke down and asked him for it one day. It was Bill, and maybe because I made a point to use it each time we met after that, one day Bill told me that he didn't consider me to be Chinese. I must have seemed different to him from his Chinese colleague in the math department, a woman who had immigrated as an adult and whose accent students complained about in their evaluations. There in the stairwell, my voice rebounding off the cinder block walls, I told Bill that I wished he *would* think about me as Chinese, surprising myself a little, and he never opened up in quite the same way with me again. Some white people don't think about you as Asian because they can turn you into an individual, like themselves.

When you look like me, what makes you Asian or not Asian are the words of others, and what makes you Asian American must be your own. Ronald Ebens tried to make Vincent Chin Asian with his words. And so maybe the first words ever spoken by an Asian American were in Chinese: "It's not fair." If not, then certainly in English: "I want justice for my son." I have been made Asian in less violent ways than Chin, although like all other Asians, especially our elders, I know there is always time. Our skin is different in this country, a cipher, not foretold like Black and white. It rolls out like paper, broad and bare for the writing. We have been written into yellow peril, to be driven out and banned and incarcerated. In the sixties, group profiles wrote us into model minorities to shame the righteous in the streets of Detroit and Chicago. And today, online, in posts shared and liked with abandon, we are written into the diseased, carriers of virus, patients zero one and all. Sometimes we write back, pinning our best English to our lapel, at the cost of our dignity, to avoid being made into something we're not. Sometimes we write a book. I went to school for the words. What I learned is that the white supremacy that makes a xenophobe and a racist can make a community on the other side. In the end, what we have in common is not a culture, not a grammar or a god, but the ignorance and hate of those who insist that we assimilate to theirs.

CHAPTER 4
AFFIRMATIVE ACTION HIRE

Until my son was born, I was the only person of color living on my block. The city of Eau Claire, Wisconsin, wasn't diverse then and still isn't. Our house resides in a ward shaped roughly like a human stomach, its western edge hugging the angular east bank of the Chippewa River, which leads the way in from the north like a great esophagus. The Chippewa flows southwest for about fifty miles until it hits the Mississippi at the Minnesota border. My father drove the cube van up from Texas to move Robin and me into our new house. The first local he met, a kind white woman who was a colleague at the university, beamed at him. "You could float from Eau Claire right into the Gulf of Mexico," she bragged. "A slow boat to China." They both laughed, friends already. Our neighborhood is known for the historic homes lining its boulevards, one Gothic Revival dating back to Reconstruction, not in this part of the country but due south, just down the river. It also encircles the state university where I teach, my short commute a ten-minute trot on a winter day, and it is a faculty enclave for that reason and others, chock-full of professors current and emeritus. Despite its lack of diversity, I get along well with my neighbors, who are friendly and generous in a way I didn't experience growing up in the north Texas suburbs.

We lived two doors down from an older white couple who had an interest in Asian people. Don and Jan sponsored a scholarship for first-year students at my university, where Don had been an accounting professor before he retired. Applicants needed to have strong high school GPAs and solid standardized test scores. They also needed to be Hmong. The Hmong were the largest racial minority group in the region, first arriving in the late seventies as refugees fleeing the Pathet Lao. Don and Jan were progressive Lutherans whose church had sponsored some of the first Hmong families in Eau Claire, Jan herself a tutor for the first Hmong graduate of my institution. Their scholarship seemed to epitomize their sense of duty as Christians and citizens, a beneficence that began as charity but was meant to eventually eliminate the need for it by becoming an education. They were the kind of people who would have welcomed any newcomer to the block, but I also wondered whether I might have stood apart as the symbol or avatar of their outreach: an Asian American neighbor who had made good, a professor and an English tutor, like themselves.

Not long after we moved into the neighborhood, Don and Jan invited us to their house to get to know us better. The conversation eventually trended in the direction of how each couple had met.

"We met in college at the University of Minnesota," Jan revealed. "Don was in graduate school." She mentioned a friend whom they had in common and how he had something to do with why she and Don began dating. "Our friend was also a student at the university but studied engineering. He became a little famous after he graduated, actually. He was part of a big lawsuit after he was rejected from medical school."

"Which university?" I asked.

"It's in California," Jan said. "Davis."

"Your friend," I began, "is Allan Bakke?"

"Yes, that's him. He won, too." Jan said this in a way that made me think she and Don agreed with the decision.

I was too stunned to press much further. Don and Jan implied that they were all still in touch.

Allan Bakke was a thirty-three-year-old white NASA engineer from Minnesota working in California when he decided that he wanted to be a doctor. In 1973, he applied to eleven medical schools. The medical school at the University of California, Davis, ran a special admissions program that reserved sixteen of one hundred spots in the freshman class for applicants "from economically and educationally disadvantaged backgrounds" that included African Americans, Chicanos, Asians, and American Indians. Since the program's authorization in 1969, no white applicants had been admitted under it, although hundreds were eligible to apply if they were "economically disadvantaged." Bakke was not considered under this program and was rejected. He wrote a letter to the school implying that he felt he had been discriminated against, but he was rejected twice more. In June 1974, he sued the regents of the University of California under the equal protection clause of the Fourteenth Amendment, his case making it to the Supreme Court in 1977. The last time the court had restricted a person's rights based on race was during World War II in its rulings against Japanese Americans, the *New York Times* reported in its April 3, 1977, profile on Bakke. Jan was right—Bakke had won. He was admitted to UC Davis's medical school, and the court also ruled that the university's special admissions program was unconstitutional because it amounted to an illegal quota system prohibited by the 1964 Civil Rights Act and the Fourteenth Amendment. Yet the court did not disqualify the use of race for admission, as many had expected it to do. Colleges could consider an applicant's race because diversity was still a "compelling goal" for the nation.

In the history of the nation's debate over granting civil rights to Black Americans, Bakke's complaint echoes past arguments and foretells modern grievances. Melvin Urofsky begins *The Affirmative Action Puzzle* with a description of the struggle over the passage of the Civil Rights Act of 1866, which was intended to protect Black Americans, especially those recently freed from enslavement, by guaranteeing that their rights were equal to those of "white citizens," including those rights "to make and enforce contracts" and "to sue." The bill earned President Andrew Johnson's veto— later overridden—with Johnson arguing that it was "made to operate in favor of the colored and against the white race." But it is a different President Johnson who is more commonly associated with the history of affirmative action; Lyndon Johnson issued an executive order in 1965 to prohibit federally contracted organizations from discriminating based on race, color, religion, and national origin. LBJ's Executive Order 11246 shored up President John F. Kennedy's Executive Order 10925 in 1961, which instructed government contractors to "take affirmative action" to ensure equal treatment of their employees along the same lines. In 1967, LBJ's Executive Order 11375 amended his prior order by adding "sex" to the list of protected categories.

Affirmative action, as conceived by Kennedy and Lyndon Johnson, was in existence for only six years—and was being implemented for even less time—before its premise was challenged in court by Marco DeFunis in 1971. While a final decision on his case was pending, DeFunis was allowed to enroll in the University of Washington Law School, which had initially rejected his application. His case reached the Supreme Court in 1974, but the court ruled the case moot because by that time DeFunis was set to graduate. Two months later, Allan Bakke launched his suit against the University of California.

I was confused. On the one hand, Don and Jan saw nothing wrong with requiring a student to be Hmong to apply for their scholarship to a state institution. On the other, they thought UC Davis should not have taken Bakke's race into consideration. Why did one situation seem like racial discrimination and not the other? Did their inconsistency have to do with Bakke being an old friend? Or with the difference between public and private money? Maybe it was because the issue of admission was not at stake in the case of the Hmong students, who had already been accepted when they applied for the scholarship. Perhaps there was no inconsistency at all to their beliefs about race, a buried constant lying underneath them both.

What I did know was that the answer didn't end with what they themselves believed. It also had to do with the broader culture and what Asian Americans meant in it, particularly to white people. There were reasons the Hmong were the largest racial minority in the region, just as there were reasons I was the only person of color living on my block. Our difference from other racial minorities inhered in how we came across as more deserving, beginning with how some of us proved ourselves in school. Asian Americans didn't need affirmative action like the others, so the story goes. We were neighbors, spouses, and colleagues without it, an overdue proof of concept. Across the country, in neighborhoods like mine, we made it possible for white Americans to look to the future, to have a past but not have to think too much about it.

* * *

In 1984, I asked my father if he would drive me to ComputerLand, the exclusive dealer for IBM personal computers in our hometown. It was tucked away in a strip mall near a corporate park next door to tax preparers and pool supply outfits, businesses that didn't rely on walk-in customers. The new software title on the shelf was hard to miss because it came in an oversized black vinyl case about the size of a component stereo receiver. Weighing about eight pounds, the package was as serious as what was inside of it. It was the *Barron's Computer Study Program for the SAT*, and it came with three double-sided floppy disks, two math and verbal workbooks, and a thick study guide that included seven full-length practice exams. It cost about $100, a lot more than any of the computer games I'd had my eye on, fitting in better alongside the expensive database and spreadsheet packages. I was going to be a junior in high school the next year and would take the SAT for the first time. I gripped the case like a stone tablet and stared at the markings on it. "This will help me get into college," I told Dad, thrusting it toward him for inspection.

"Good," he said without looking at it, and took it to the counter.

My parents helped us children with our homework until about the fourth grade, which is when we stopped asking them questions and took over our educations for good. Dad completed a couple of years of secondary school in Qingdao before the Communist Revolution cut short his formal education. My mother graduated from Maryknoll Convent School in Hong Kong and took some classes at the University of Washington. I didn't bother them with trigonometry or *Animal Farm*. Dad liked how the SAT software was like a private tutor that took you step by step through a solution. He stood behind me and looked over my shoulder at the colorful geometric patterns being drawn onto the monitor screen. He'd sold his beloved Hasselblad to afford the PC, and I think he liked seeing the investment pay off before his eyes. The reality that a single test could determine so much of your future did not seem odd or unfair to him. When he was a kid, the civil service exams of imperial China weren't yet ancient history, and he told me stories about the lengths to which boys like his grandfather had gone to keep themselves awake to study for them. He liked the idea that how far you could go was determined by your own merit— how hard you were willing to study and how much leisure time you were willing to cede. He stuck around when I was taking the math portion of the exam and usually walked away during the verbal, bored by the analogies.

The University of Texas admitted me due in no small part to my SAT score, which rated a scholarship from its school of engineering as well. I had logged dozens of hours with the prep software and had taken all of its model SAT exams. My parents praised my hard work, as did my friends' parents, who were white and had college degrees themselves. The SAT, I discovered soon enough, was not hard work. You did not learn math or English from it. If you aced it, it was because you learned a more basic truth, a structure. The software taught me how to see it in a way my parents never could. The SAT was an exercise in time management, a two-minute drill. If you couldn't round off digits or skim syllables, you were guaranteed not to finish. You never gave each possible choice its due—you tossed three of them by instinct and did the minimum to decide between the final two. You shot ahead to the next question the second you knew you couldn't do this, returning only if you had the luxury to dawdle. The value of each question to you was relative. They were not deserving of equal time. Knowing this made beating the SAT not hard work but the opposite. It was a confidence game, and the test was the mark. If you could get into its head, you could get it to give you everything it had.

But in the minds of white Americans, gaming the SAT did not make Asian American students like me into people who knew how to work the system, like welfare cheats. It made us seem more deserving. Our scores quantified our merit as salaries seemed to, which made making comparisons feel natural. In *No Longer Separate, Not Yet Equal*, the researchers Thomas Espenshade and Alexandria Radford presented their findings that Asian Americans scoring a perfect 1,600 had the same chances of acceptance to elite institutions as white peers who scored 1,460 and Black peers who scored 1,150, a conclusion that has defined the ongoing narrative of the deserving Asian American. Since then, in any given feature story about affirmative action, Asian American students appear front and center. We are posed like our ancestors whose photos adorn our family shrines, staring off into the distance with faces of grim resolve, never smiling, as if to say, "I sacrificed." Our SAT scores follow our names like the birth years of a line of kings—1,480 to 1,600. It's easy to believe in the objectivity of these numbers, more decent for making comparisons than an intelligence quotient, which enough people take seriously too. Never mind how often researchers have concluded that the SAT is better at predicting the family income of students than their college success. We can work the system and seem deserving at the same time.

The SAT has done more than get Asian Americans into college. It has made us whiter.

*   *   *

Asians in the United States have taken many routes to pass for white, some leading to the Supreme Court. In 1922, the Japanese immigrant Takao Ozawa said that he should be allowed to naturalize based on the Nationality Act of 1790. His brief asserted that the law used the word "white" "in counterdistinction from black, and 'free white persons' included all who were not black. . . . 'White person,' . . . means a person without negro blood." Justice George Sutherland spoke for the court when he wrote that Ozawa wasn't white because he wasn't a "Caucasian." Only a few months later, the court heard the case of another Asian immigrant, Bhagat Singh Thind, a Sikh man from India, who also sued to naturalize. Thind's lawyers made an anthropological argument, claiming that their client's status as a high-caste Hindu from the Punjab region technically made him a Caucasian and a member of the "Aryan race": "The high-class Hindu regards the aboriginal Indian Mongoloid in the same manner as the American regards the negro, speaking from a matrimonial standpoint." Sutherland represented the court's unanimous opinion that "Caucasian" should not be understood in scientific but "common" terms: white. And Indians, like Japanese, were not white. Ozawa and Thind held that they were white because they were not Black.

In time, the country agreed that Asians were not Black. The model minority stereotype was formed in the fifties and emerged in the sixties, springing like wise Athena from a powerful brow. "Success Story, Japanese-American Style" appeared in the *New York Times Magazine* in 1966. Historical injustice created "problem minorities," laments the sociologist William Petersen, minorities who suffered from "self-defeating apathy or a hatred so all-consuming as to be self-destructive." Not all minorities were a problem, however. "By any criterion of good citizenship that we choose," the article explains, "the Japanese Americans are better than any other group in our society, including native-born whites." Later that year, *U.S. News and World Report* echoed Petersen with its take on Chinese Americans. "Success Story of One Minority Group in U.S." opens with a lede like a blockbuster's voice-over: "At a time when Americans are awash in worry over the plight of racial minorities—" The article goes on to state, "Still being taught in Chinatown is the old idea that people should depend on their own efforts—not a welfare check—in order to reach America's 'promised land.'" As the historian Ellen D. Wu recounts in *The Color of Success: Asian Americans and the Origins of the Model Minority*, political reporters and pundits spun Senator Daniel Inouye's appearance at the 1968 Democratic National Convention in Chicago to push the idea that past racial discrimination was no barrier to success in America—this despite Inouye's keynote address that methodically argued that the situation of Asians like himself could not and should not be compared to that of Black Americans, who had faced the "systematic racist deprivation" of Jim Crow. Even so, Lyndon Johnson suggested that Hubert Humphrey select Inouye as his running mate for his model minority bona fides. Resistance to the civil rights movement created the model minority stereotype, which was never truly about Asian Americans. It was another monument to white supremacy, erected, as usual, in backlash to the prospect of Black social equality.

The month I left for college, *Time* magazine put six smiling Asian American students on the cover of its August 31, 1987, issue. "The New Whiz Kids" began by acknowledging the model minority stereotype but was mostly a profile of Asian American "superstudents." My high school had its share of superstudents and whiz kids. It crowned a Taiwanese American valedictorian and then seemingly couldn't decide between Asians, choosing two salutatorians: a Korean American and an Indian American. My friend's sister said that there should be two valedictorians because it wasn't fair to make white students like her compete against Asians. She would have made academics our own segregated prom.

I wasn't a true whiz kid like the others, but I was close enough. The cover story made it seem like we were superstudents because our parents made us that way. But the story made us that way too. "The largely successful Asian-American experience is a challenging counterpoint to the charges that U.S. schools are now producing less-educated mainstream students and failing to help underclass blacks and Hispanics," its author concludes. It was still important for us not to be Black. We were like the corporate tycoons whose faces usually appeared on the cover of *Time* to prove that the system worked for those worthy of it.

Ozawa and Thind said that they were white not because their blood was Asian but because their blood was not Black. Magazines and newspapers that came later implied that it wasn't our blood but our culture that made us not Black, especially in school. Yet many Asians got average and even bad grades and still were seen as not Black. Some were refugees whose parents didn't arrive with degrees from universities in Taipei or Seoul. The Cambodians and Vietnamese had fled genocide like the Hmong student tutored by my neighbor Jan. They were not quite as white as our Taiwanese American valedictorian but still not Black. They were perceived as trying hard, even if their GPAs did not reflect their lofty ambitions. Their bad grades did not make them bad students. Perhaps they avoided being thought of as bad students because they were grateful to be in America and did what they were told. To be bad students, they had to complain that things were tougher for them because they were still learning standard English, or because their parents couldn't advocate for them, or because they didn't have parents anymore, or because they missed their people, or because they learned America was not a nation of immigrants after all, which was another way to say they learned about Native genocide and Black chattel slavery. They had to complain. If they complained, they implied that the fault was not all theirs. If they complained, they implied that the past mattered to who they were. Affirmative action also made people think about the past, namely slavery. Being accepted into the model minority meant that our ethnicity was more important than race, which is to say that our culture was more important than history.

*   *   *

In the ninth grade, we took a test that our teacher told us was not for a grade. "There are no wrong answers, people," he said more than once. The test would analyze our responses and match us with the best possible career to suit our talents and interests. Because we had bubbled in a Scantron form, I expected the results right away, but it took weeks to get them back from the company. I was anxious over that time because no one told us that the test could be wrong despite there being no wrong answers. When the day came and our teacher passed back our results, I learned I was supposed to be an actuary. I didn't know what actuaries did and was disappointed when I read that they worked at insurance companies because they were good at math. I didn't like how their work seemed to put them behind the scenes instead of out front with other people. I didn't mention it to my parents. When I told my friends' parents the result, one pursed his lips and nodded. "It's a good career for you," he said. "Very stable." Later, when I agreed with the test that I was good at math and decided to be an engineer, which seemed like a less anonymous occupation than actuary, he said the same thing. No one ever asked me why I wanted to be an engineer. I was like the friendly white girls in class whom nobody asked why they wanted to be a teacher or a nurse.

I was a bad college student, it turned out. At the orientation for the school of engineering, a white professor stood at the front of the auditorium and told us to look at the student to our left and then at the one to our right. "One of them won't be here by the end," he said, meaning failures. I laughed at his joke, which made us pity and even scorn the unqualified and undeserving. Half the people in the room were Asian like me, but the professor made me dislike them the way my friend's sister disliked them. I survived my first semester but strung together mostly Cs and Ds after that. I was put on academic warning and then lost my scholarship. It was strange that the standardized tests had been wrong about me. It would be years before I would know what my race had to do with my education. The sociologist Jennifer Lee coined the term "stereotype promise" to describe how some students—Asian Americans, mostly—perform better in school because of positive stereotypes of their academic potential. It's the counterpoint to the concept of "stereotype threat," popularized by the psychologist Claude Steele, which explains how low expectations predict poor performance. Stereotype promise didn't work for me. I wasn't going to be an engineer, and I was still Chinese. I also realized that I had been hoping that being Chinese would not matter as much to others if I were an engineer. Our jobs were supposed to be who we were to white people. The magazines had implied that being a bad Asian student was the same as being a bad American, which was the same as being bad. I was a person of color who was assumed to be more competent because of my race but wasn't—the opposite of the model minority stereotype.

Deep down I knew I wasn't qualified for the school of engineering. I couldn't pass a required course in network theory even after taking it twice. Computer science wasn't the same as ComputerLand. I understood how people could be qualified or not qualified for something, even though I was the latter. Allan Bakke didn't want to talk about being qualified or not qualified, however, but about being *more* qualified. Like GPAs, the SAT made it easy to think and talk about being more qualified than others. But adding the "more" let those on hiring or admissions committees move the goalposts based on qualitative standards—their own. Asians like me spent our youths becoming more qualified. For what, we didn't know. In high school I had volunteered at a local hospital where my friend's mother worked because she told my friend and me it would help us get into college. Volunteering showed that we cared about the less fortunate. At home, I modeled the beige polyester smock the hospital gave me with my name on it, making me one of the more fortunate, I suppose. "But they don't pay you?" was all my father said.

Being more qualified meant volunteering, internships, studying abroad, going on mission trips—anything that took time that you might have spent working an after-school job or helping support your family in another way. We weren't becoming more qualified for an occupation, which was the reason for the test with no wrong answers. We were becoming more qualified to have an occupation around white people.

I didn't need affirmative action to get into college, but I needed it to get out. After changing my major to English, I spent my last two years studying literature and hoping that I could write it. Almost all the students in my English classes were white, as were the teaching assistants and professors, so different from the engineering school. We rarely talked about race in class because literature was supposed to be about universals. I didn't know to think about too many white people in a classroom as a problem because it had never occurred to me to do so. I was more used to thinking, *There are a lot of Asians here*, and that awareness usually making wherever I was seem a little worse, even though I was one of them. It is the same racist calculus that, after a point, makes the quality of a school seem directly proportional to how many white students attend. In the *Bakke* decision, Justice Lewis Powell had agreed that a "diverse student body" was still a "compelling goal" for the nation, which meant racially homogenous classrooms limited the quality of the education, which limited the vitality of the nation. Being Chinese helped to get me into graduate school in spite of Allan Bakke. The reason for affirmative action was now the need for more diversity instead of the need for less discrimination. I didn't know it yet, but I was supposed to diversify my classes as a graduate student in Eugene and Ann Arbor.

Because I was Asian American and good at English, the University of Michigan awarded me the Rackham Merit Fellowship for Historically Underrepresented Groups. It was an affirmative action award, unlike the engineering scholarship that came with my SAT score. Not long after I graduated, its name was shortened to just the "Rackham Merit Fellowship." Perhaps enough people complained that the old name carried a stigma that the word "merit" couldn't lift. Or maybe the change had to do with Michigan voters deciding to end affirmative action in the state in 2006. I didn't mind the original name. I liked how it made people think about the past. "Historically underrepresented" was code for "racially oppressed" that did not force anyone to say who or what was doing the oppressing, only who was being underrepresented. But the words were at least a gesture, and dropping them not only made affirmative action seem like something to be ashamed of but put the shame on those of us who needed affirmative action, where it always had been, rather than on those who made us need its justice. The words were also missing from the test with no wrong answers. The missing words spoke to what racism had to do with the jobs we held, a future we were led to believe was up to our own tastes and personalities. The missing words explained stable canons and stable careers. They were why it wasn't enough for us to think that we were good at something, even if we were right.

*   *   *

I am the quintessential affirmative action hire. I don't mean that I was unqualified for my job or any less qualified than a white applicant, which is what the insult was originally supposed to imply. I mean that my race likely had something to do with my getting the job I have now and that it continued to matter even after I was hired. What you make of this probably has to do with what the word "race" means to you. The job description called for a professor of English with a specialization in "ethnic American literature." I can't say how much the search committee expected that an "ethnic American" would teach "ethnic American literature." It certainly wasn't required for the position, not after *Bakke*. The search attracted more than two hundred applicants, many of them "nonethnic Americans," I have to think. "American" literature was assumed to be white literature, just as "American" people were assumed to be white people, neither marked. I was happy to get the job however I could. It is still hard for me to imagine another job that more plainly suggested how much my race mattered in getting it. Maybe, I thought, "professor of ethnic American literature" was the rare kind of job where not being white was perceived as an asset. This turned out not to be true at all, of course, but I got the benefit of the doubt more often than my Black and Latino colleagues in other departments, especially the women, who were further away from whiteness than I was. They were the ones more likely to be perceived as affirmative action hires by their colleagues and students. The only way any of us could escape the suspicion was to be white.

At my university, we didn't have many professors who could be perceived as affirmative action hires because of their race because we didn't have many professors of color. One reason was the debate over what counted as diversity. At a faculty retreat one summer, I gave a presentation on our struggle to recruit and retain diverse faculty. A white geology professor insisted that there was no difference, diversity-wise, between a Black scholar from Nigeria and a Black scholar from the United States. A white history professor from a former Soviet satellite argued that the kind of diversity that we were really missing these days was the ideological kind. When I tried to return the discussion on diversity to race in the United States by suggesting that structural racism was behind the numbers, a white political science professor frowned. "That's a very serious allegation," he said. On a search committee in my own department, after I pointed out that writing programs lacked diversity, a white colleague cited a survey showing that atheists like himself were, in fact, the most disfavored group in the country. Affirmative action was still about race, despite the poor state that Allan Bakke had left it in. But so many of my white colleagues did what they could not to have to talk about race. They had discovered that the best way not to have to talk about race was to talk about nationality, or censorship, or religion, or my insolence.

Many colleagues didn't talk about race if they could talk about ethnicity instead, it being easier to celebrate difference than to contemplate it, because then you didn't have to talk about power. "Ethnic Americans" didn't need affirmative action because they had no race. A few students were surprised that their "ethnic American literature" class focused so much on racism and not on culture. I said that what made characters seem ethnic to them—how they made a living, how they stuck together, etc.—was related to their oppression. The immigrant father in the autobiography we read together was stern to his children not solely because he was a Confucian but because he feared for their safety in this country. My students began the semester believing that the father could be Chinese without also being not white. But in time they learned not to confuse race and ethnicity, which may have been the payoff that Justice Powell had in mind. The difference between the two, wrote the legal scholar Harlon Dalton, was that ethnic groups did not need one another to exist. Races existed only in relation to one another. What made me an Asian American wasn't the language my parents spoke or our holiday dinner; it was my place in a hierarchy between white and Black. The status of your skin wasn't absolute but relative to that of your neighbor, like an exam score graded on a curve.

For years, nobody talked about white people having a race and what it had to do with getting jobs at my university. Many were hired on to the tenure track because their partners were already on it, touring the campus at their formal interview the way someone would tour their own house. Some faced no competition at all. I recall a conversation with a white professor named Mitchell whose father had retired from the university before I arrived. I liked Mitchell because he knew that he had a race. He admitted that he was recruited by word of mouth, without a search. "People already knew me because of my dad," he said. Every fall, department chairs kick off our first college meeting by introducing their new faculty. "You'll be happy to know that he's one of us," a chair in the natural sciences began one year, placing his arm around a younger white man. The young man grew up in the next state over, he went on to say, and already had plenty in common with "us." Some years brought in newly minted PhDs who had attended our university as undergraduates. Older colleagues beamed at these new arrivals like they were their own children. I wondered why these career paths told a success story for so many and not the opposite. We spoke of our accomplishments with pride or prudence depending on whether we knew we had a race.

Each semester, I ask an auditorium full of future teachers when affirmative action began. Occasionally one of them guesses right that it's a trick question. The trick is that white is a race, meaning that state-sponsored racial preference is as old as whiteness. The argument made by the universities defending affirmative action in the DeFunis and Bakke cases was that their policies were not unconstitutional because they sought to remedy centuries of racial discrimination against those groups who benefited from the policy. But discrimination does not exist without preference, just as "underrepresented" does not exist without "overrepresented." Since the colonial era, affirmative action for white people has existed under the names of other policies, as Ira Katznelson argues in *When Affirmative Action Was White*. Among others, these included "freedom dues" for indentured servants, the Nationality Act of 1790, the Homestead Act, and the GI Bill of Rights, all of which invented the white man only to praise him. Yet the words "affirmative action" did not get most of the students to think about white men, maybe because 1790 was before 1961, the year that Kennedy's executive order coined the term. Yet neither did "affirmative action" get them to think about white women, the group gaining the most from it since 1967, the year LBJ added "sex" as a protected category. In general, the white students did not think enough about their fathers and their grandfathers, nor their mothers and grandmothers, as white people in this way. They did not think enough about *themselves* as white people in this way, as heirs to such preference. They did not see their whiteness in history. Their whiteness began in 1978 because of Allan Bakke, who transformed it from a birthright into a detail, a color among colors in the eyes of the law. In this new era, he absolved the penitent of their guilt and anticipated the persecution to come.

*   *   *

Jennifer Gratz was born in 1977, the year that Bakke brought his case before the Supreme Court. Gratz, a white woman, applied for admission to the University of Michigan in 1995 but was denied. Two years later, she sued the university, taking her case against its affirmative action policy to the Supreme Court in 2003, the first white person to do so since Bakke. Like him, she won. The court ruled that the university's holistic admission system—which assigned a numerical value to an applicant's race as part of a point system—was unconstitutional. Gratz went on to become executive director of the Michigan Civil Rights Initiative, which, in 2006, successfully brought a referendum to ballot that ended race-based affirmative action in the state. On the same day that the court ruled in *Gratz v. Bollinger*, it also ruled in *Grutter v. Bollinger*, in which another white woman, Barbara Grutter, sued the University of Michigan Law School for discriminating against her as a white person. Grutter lost, and the court upheld the Bakke precedent, maintaining that diversity was still a "compelling interest." Despite the twin high-profile cases, affirmative action had not fundamentally changed since *Bakke*. White people could still be the victims of racial discrimination, but race still mattered in decision-making because of the purported benefits of diversity. The fight to end affirmative action required a new strategy.

When I was a graduate student at Michigan, I received an email inviting me to a meeting for Asian American students. I recognized some of my friends there, and the refreshments led us to assume it was a social gathering. Before too long, however, the organizers of this meeting explained their purpose in bringing us together: to convince us that the university discriminated against Asian Americans by giving preferences to Black, Latino, and Native American applicants. Asian Americans needed better grades and test scores to be given the same consideration, they told us, egging us on to air our own resentments. My fellowship said that I was "historically underrepresented" like Black, Latino, and Native American students, but the organizers of this meeting said that I was not like them but like white people. I left the meeting angry at the organizers for trying to use Asian Americans as a wedge to divide people of color. It was another chapter in the model minority myth, I thought, with Asians cast as honorary white people.

In 2008, the University of Texas rejected the application of a high school student from Sugar Land, Texas. Four years later, Abigail Fisher, a white woman, sued my alma mater for racial discrimination. Despite her less competitive GPA and SAT score, Fisher, in her brief to the Supreme Court, argued that her "academic credentials exceeded those of many admitted minority candidates." Fisher lost before the court, twice, partly because of her mediocre qualifications. Yet her lawsuit was notable for how it changed course from those of Bakke, Gratz, and Grutter, which had painted only white people as victims. The University of Texas "employs race in admissions decisions to the detriment of Asian Americans, thus subjecting them to the same inequality as White applicants," read the brief, which mentioned Asian Americans twenty-two times. In his fifty-one-page dissent to the court's 2016 decision against Fisher, Justice Samuel Alito mentioned white people eleven times and Asian Americans sixty-two times. Alito was arguing white Americans into victimhood by proxy. White people, it seemed, were now honorary Asians.

Fisher v. University of Texas did not end the fight against affirmative action nor the prominence of Asian Americans in it. Its architect was Edward Blum, an activist best known for orchestrating *Shelby County v. Holder*, the Supreme Court case that ended provisions of the 1965 Voting Rights Act. Blum founded Students for Fair Admissions (SFFA) with Fisher and her father to recruit new anti–affirmative action plaintiffs. Blum knew that something had to change, even before the Supreme Court loss. "I needed Asian plaintiffs," he explained. SFFA launched a campaign seeking Asian American students denied admission to competitive public and private institutions. By 2014, SFFA had built a case with Asian American plaintiffs (who asked to remain anonymous) to sue Harvard in US federal court. These plaintiffs had stronger academic credentials than Fisher and, it seemed, additional standing tied directly to their race. SFFA argued that Harvard engaged in racial "balancing" to maintain a fixed share of Asian American students by lowering their rating in the "personal" category of the holistic admission process. Harvard, SFFA implied, held Asian American applicants to the stereotype of the introverted nerd.

Blum reminded me of the anti–affirmative action organizers at Michigan in the nineties. *Students for Fair Admissions v. Harvard* further divided Asian Americans over the issue of affirmative action. While the majority of Asian Americans support affirmative action, Blum appealed to an organized and vocal wing of recent immigrants, especially from China. One woman was photographed on the steps of the Supreme Court holding a sign that read ASIAN AMERICAN AGAINST DISCRIMINATION. In 2015, in a San Jose megachurch called the Point, Blum roiled five hundred members of the Silicon Valley Chinese Association (SVCA) with his account of Harvard's "personal" rating. He implied that

Asian Americans could be the group that ended racial discrimination in higher education. The founder of the SVCA, Alex Chen, told the *New Yorker* that the purpose of his activism was to do "something for future generations." He added, "If we are for ourselves, we do not need to do this." Despite the opening statement of SFFA lead attorney Adam Mortara that "the future of affirmative action is not on trial," many supporters of affirmative action believed that Blum and his backers were using Asian Americans only to begin a larger assault on the consideration of race in federal funding. In this movement, Asian Americans were cast as the new civil rights pioneers.

In October 2019, the federal judge Allison Burroughs ruled that Harvard did not discriminate against Asian Americans. SFFA had lost again but was here to stay. In October 2022, the Supreme Court heard Blum's case against Harvard and a similar one that Blum had filed against the University of North Carolina.

*   *   *

In 1971, when my family landed in the United States for good, my father was like Alex Chen in one crucial way. He wouldn't have been an activist like the younger man and might have mocked him for his hubris, but he would have understood why Chen had set his sights directly on the future. Like other Asians of his generation, my father left Communist revolutions and European colonialism behind him just as the 1965 Hart-Celler Act made obsolete the 1924 Johnson-Reed Act. The year 1971 was the first on record that immigrants from Asia outnumbered those from Europe, according to editor and journalist Jia Lynn Yang in *One Mighty and Irresistible Tide: The Epic Struggle over American Immigration, 1924–1965*. Hart-Celler scrapped racist immigration quotas, favoring those seeking to reunite families, those "who are members of the professions," and those "who are capable of performing specified skilled or unskilled labor." My father listed his occupation as "master tailor" on his application, and since we had no family who were citizens to sponsor us, his craft was enough, apparently, to get us through the door. Dad did like to tinker with electronics like his prized Zenith shortwave radio that he tuned to scratchy Chinese voices late at night. "I think I would be a good engineer if my father let me go to college," he said after I was accepted to UT. The closest my father came to that was wiring the porcelain lamps he sold. His two younger brothers had graduated from universities around Dallas. It made sense to me then why he had traded his camera for the IBM, which he was proud of but never truly knew how to operate without my help. I think it was enough for him just to be a part of something new.

Asian Americans are divided over affirmative action not because we are divided over race but because we are divided over the future and the past. After I needed affirmative action to get out of college, my parents couldn't understand why I cared so much about the past and especially about the parts that didn't seem to concern me. "People like us were excluded from the country for a long time," I explained.

"So what?" was all my father would say, because he wasn't stuck in China at the moment.

"People deserve civil rights . . ." I continued, trailing off when I saw the look on Dad's face. He didn't have to say that life wasn't fair and that it was folly to try to make it so. He and my mother completely shut down whenever I brought up rights for Black people. They didn't care to think about their own history at the time, let alone that of strangers. Why choose to make someone else's problems their own? They had crammed for a citizenship test not to learn history but to become citizens.

Their lives in America had made them like Chen in other ways. People like Chen didn't need to go down as civil rights heroes and probably didn't even see themselves in such consequential terms. They weren't interested in making history or even talking about it. They fought affirmative action on behalf of their families to come.

Yet Chen's sense of history was born with Allan Bakke's victory too. It did not include Hart-Celler in 1965 or Appomattox a century before. Chen arrived on an H-1B visa, not bartering for computer chips like my father but engineering them. Edward Blum projected a future that had every reason to look bright for Chen and his family if not for the discrimination against them. Blum knew that Asians didn't choose to come to a country only to denounce it. He knew that they wanted to speculate on the future, not to brood over the past. Blum sued Harvard under Title VI of the Civil Rights Act of 1964. Civil rights were now for people like Chen, he implied, and not for those they were invented for, even though 1964 was before 1965, the year Hart-Celler was signed into law. Congressman Emanuel Celler himself had fought Jim Crow before he fought Johnson-Reed. The Civil Rights Act of 1964 had been won for people like me by people unlike me. It had been dreamed of upon the National Mall and not inside a suburban mall. It had been pulled from a Baptist church in Birmingham and not a megachurch in San Jose. Edward Blum dreamed about the future too. His goal wasn't to relieve personal injury. It wasn't even to shame Harvard. It was to turn "race" from an idea from our history back into a word from the dictionary, its meaning good only for memorization.

*   *   *

When my son was a few years old, and I was no longer the only person of color on my block, our neighbor Jan dropped by to give him a present. It was a colorful, oversized children's book by Richard Scarry—*Best Word Book Ever*, or something along those lines. Jan and Don were good neighbors, and it made sense that they had chosen a book as a present. Their own children were grown and impressively accomplished, out of the house and scattered across the country. We chatted about where Jacob might go to preschool the next year— their church had an excellent 4K program, Jan said—and what my hopes were for him. Before becoming a father, I hadn't thought about the future in that way because it had been only Robin and me for so long. Imagining the future with Jan and other friends felt open and expansive, a little heady. I could understand Alex Chen's optimism better even if I didn't share his politics. "He'll be out on his own before you know it," Jan said. "Off to college."

"Maybe he's not college material," I joked, the way Chinese fathers might talk about their sons to protect them from jealous gods, too much of the college talk coming from Chinese American fathers lately. Today the children find ways to protect themselves from higher powers. Some mixed-race children with an Asian parent check off only one box—"white"—when reporting their race on college applications. Maybe some already thought about themselves that way, college or not.

Jan made a face, then smiled politely. The public schools in town were excellent, she told me. We complained about our property taxes but agreed that we got our money's worth. All I knew about the nearby high school was that it had stuck a terrifying model of its mascot on its roof, a fiberglass bald eagle the size of a pterodactyl, named Old Abe. The real Old Abe was a war eagle carried into battle by the Eighth Wisconsin at Vicksburg and in other Civil War campaigns, the great bird supposedly earning salutes from men like Generals Ulysses S. Grant and William T. Sherman. When I first moved to Wisconsin, I was glad to settle in a state that had fought for the Union—with monuments like Old Abe, no less—unlike Texas, where Abigail Fisher and I grew up. But it was strange that a state that had ostensibly fought for Black people had so few of them in it. It was strange that the Mississippi that rolled through here was the same river that ended in Louisiana. Parts of the upper Midwest chose not to segregate by race so much as banish by it, their landscape dotted with sundown towns. Black elders dictated their unwritten rules to their children with the ferocity of tiger parents. And well into the twentieth century, government-run agencies in Wisconsin systematically separated Native American families—from the

Ojibwe, Ho-Chunk, and Oneida nations, among others—
removing thousands of children from their homes and communities and relocating them into boarding schools, which
forced their assimilation into the dominant white culture.
Our mascots around the state were war eagles, yes, but also
warriors and chiefs.

Jan and I hadn't spoken about Allan Bakke again after
that night years ago. I didn't need to hear the reason she and
Don felt that race should matter for their scholarship winners but not for their college friend, and I wouldn't know
how to ask about it and remain cordial. I hoped I knew the
answer anyway.

It was because they were supporting dreams.

At the March on Washington in 1963, Martin Luther
King Jr. spoke about his dream of a future. His Black dream
was so powerful that some white people felt left out, believing that their own dreams were somehow threatened by
King's vision. Allan Bakke decided that affirmative action
wouldn't stand in the way of his dream of becoming a
doctor, which it never did. Bakke went home to Minnesota
to practice anesthesiology instead of rocket science. Not
all dreams shoot for the moon. Privilege turned desires
into dreams, disappointment into injustice. Abigail Fisher
blamed affirmative action for ending her dream of being a
Texas Longhorn, a tradition in her family, which it never

did. Her grades, not her race, had sealed her fate. Fisher
went on to earn a degree in finance from Louisiana State
University. Jennifer Gratz, who defeated the University of
Michigan in court and then affirmative action at the polls,
said that "the dream of the 1964 Civil Rights Act was color-
blind government." White people like her transposed MLK's
dream of the day when white people would be free of what
their need for race had done to them with their own dream
of the day when they would be free of Black people talking
about race in front of them. It mixed up Black dreams for
the future with white dreams for the past.

After 1965, Asians like my parents came bearing their
own dreams for the future, which were not like Black
dreams because white people did not have to think about
their own past when listening to them. In the seventies and
eighties, Asians like the Hmong came to the United States
because their dream of a homeland in Laos had vanished
with the Americans in 1975. They had waged a secret war
that had sent their children to battle instead of to school.
They were political refugees and should have made white
people think about their past but didn't. The local newspapers printed their pictures and stories as long as their
dreams were about the future, like college, and not about
the past, like war. The Hmong past in Laos and Thailand
was not even a footnote to the Vietnam War in the history

courses taught at my university when I first arrived there. I was also surprised to learn that I was not technically an affirmative action hire after all. I fell into a category called "non-preferred minority," which very often included Asian Americans. In retrospect, that term accurately described my place in the mix. The state drew a line of privilege between East Asian Americans like myself and Southeast Asian Americans like the Hmong. I was disappointed, but not like Bakke, not because I thought the other Asian Americans were getting things that I wasn't. I was disappointed because we didn't have more in common.

If the spirit of affirmative action is to live on, it will be because Asian Americans see how our dreams are bound up with Black dreams, even in how we have come to talk about ourselves. "Southeast Asian" is only another way to say "war," like "African" in "African American." The words were meant to refer to groups but instead refer to guilts, those dwelling in the white conscience. They do not say where we came from but where those who would divide us went and did not belong.

CHAPTER 5
LOVING STORY

The most famous wedding between a Chinese man and a white American woman occurred in 1875. As the historian Emma Jinhua Teng recounts in her book *Eurasian*, the *New York Times* ran a piece on the celebrated affair under the headline YUNG WING MARRIES A CONNECTICUT LADY. It was remarkable to me that Yung Wing got top billing over his nameless bride. A Daughter of the American Revolution, Mary Louise Kellogg belonged to a prominent Connecticut family descended from *Mayflower* settlers that ran in the same social circles as Samuel Clemens (aka Mark Twain). Teng complicates the common take on unions between Chinese men and white women in nineteenth-century America, showing how the perception of interracial marriage as a social threat was only part of the story. The account of Yung's marriage to Kellogg was the bookend to the sensationalist narratives of degraded miscegenation between lustful "Chinamen" and desperate Irishwomen.

Indeed, local periodicals and histories framed Yung as quite a catch: the first Chinese graduate of Yale and the Christian founder of the Chinese Educational Mission (CEM), an important collaboration between imperial China's Qing dynasty government and New England schools and colleges. Those commending the marriage usually did so because they saw it as a positive step toward the assimilation of an educated class of Chinese immigrants, which included their conversion to Christianity. (When CEM graduate Yan Phou Lee wed Elizabeth Maude Jerome in 1887, the *Hartford Daily Courant* ran the simple headline YAN PHOU LEE ASSIMILATES.)

Before long, however, Chinese officials grew suspicious of the CEM curriculum and of Yung himself, believing that both had become too Westernized. Yung had naturalized as an American citizen and wore Western clothes and hair, ridding himself of the queue that symbolized loyalty to the Manchu emperor. As tensions came to a head, a rival at the CEM called for its disbanding, reporting back to Chinese authorities that he saw "some of the Chinese boys walking home from church in the company of American women," Teng writes. In 1881, despite appeals from Mark Twain and Ulysses S. Grant, the Chinese government closed the CEM, recalling all its students, and Yung too was called back to serve in China, leaving behind his wife and their two children in Connecticut.

I doubt that anything would have changed for me had the CEM endured and more of its graduates gone on to marry white women. The objection China had to interracial marriage probably mattered less in its decision to withdraw than the insult it suffered when military academies at West Point and Annapolis chose not to admit CEM students. The prospect for Chinese immigrants in America was rapidly dimming. The Chinese Exclusion Act would be passed the year after Yung returned to China, and the United States was entering into the period known as the "Nadir," the lowest point in race relations, marked by terrorism and state violence directed against Black Americans, Native Americans, Chinese, and other non-white people. Yung Wing piques me because he feared that his race would keep him a single man in this country. In his journal, the Reverend Joseph Twichell, who married Yung and Kellogg, notes that Yung had believed "that there was no Chinese woman whom he would marry and no American lady who would marry him." Yung may have come to believe what his Congregationalist sponsors and family did, which was that who he was in this country depended on who his wife was. His intellectual gifts and reserve of cultural capital shielded him somewhat from the curses of Sinophobic stereotypes at the time, but he too fell victim to the dehumanizing meanings of non-white identity circulating during the Nadir. In

1902, while he was in China, his American citizenship was revoked under the Naturalization Act of 1870.

I want to believe that Yung Wing loved Mary Louise Kellogg, who died young and did not accompany him on his return to China partly because of her declining health. Nothing in the historical record leads me to think that he didn't, and a tender account of her last years in his 1909 memoir, *My Life in China and America*, reads sincere. After being away from his wife and sons for eighteen months, Yung returned to the United States to minister to her, and he vowed never to "leave [his family] again under any conditions whatever." Kellogg's death, he writes, "made a great void in my after-life, which was irreparable." It's curious to me how Yung came to believe that a Chinese woman was a bad match for him but also that China was his true home, before and after he was returned there, a true patriot. Pressured from both sides of the Pacific, he must have had little choice over where he could make that home. But perhaps any cultural allegiances he had sworn to this country evanesced along with his celebrated marriage to Kellogg, the Puritan anchor of his American claim. Or perhaps he wanted to say how he had reconciled both loves but didn't have the words he needed or didn't think that anyone else would care.

* * *

Interracial marriages like those of Yung Wing and Yan Phou Lee were discouraged and later prohibited in imperial and early republican China, not because of the American taboo of miscegenation, Teng explains, but because they ran counter to the traditional practice of arranged marriage. The fears were that American white women either would not return to China with their Western-educated husbands or would not uphold Confucian familial obligations if they did. I don't remember exactly when my father told me that the marriage of his parents had been arranged, but I was old enough to be ashamed about it. Dad loved his mother more than his father and told me how nai nai despised living with ah yeh's parents, who expected her to care for them like a good daughter-in-law. Other than that, however, the fact that his parents never loved each other didn't really seem to bother him. Although I never knew my ah yeh and nai nai very well, I suspect that they grew to hate rather than love each other. Their marriage may have been a reason my mother's family, living a respectable life in Hong Kong, looked down on my father and his family, refugees crossing the border from China only months ahead of the inevitable Communist victory in 1949. "Did your parents have an arranged marriage too?" I asked my mother. "No!" she snapped. "They were in love." She showed me her own marriage license, which bore the fancy leonine heraldry of the crown colony. At the time,

I liked seeing it because I probably thought that the British would allow marriage only between people who wanted to be married to each other. But I could be given a pass for thinking like that. In the West, in so many ways, you learned that people got married because they fell in love, not because they were told to, and if you were especially romantic, you believed that the person you married was the only one you could have. Because love was special, so were you.

I wonder what it must have been like for my parents in Hong Kong not to have to think about their race factoring into love and attraction, processes that were complicated enough as it was. You might be too poor, or too fat, or too short, or too bald, or too old, but you didn't have to think about a trait that could get you confused with someone you didn't even know and in a way that you didn't like.

I used to feel that I was replaceable to any potential partner in this country, or at least my body was, since so much of our meaning as Asians here was bound up in our appearance. For most of my adolescence, I was short for my age, at least relative to teenagers in this country, and merely having to look up into the eyes of a girl I liked was enough, in my mind, to close the door on whatever future we might have, a verdict that I assumed she shared as well. But it was my face that led me to feel this way most profoundly, my square black bangs—looking bowl cut no matter what I tried in front of the mirror—capping off a moonlike aspect that struck me as generic even though it routinely floated across a sea of white faces. For a long time, certainly while I was still dating or wanting to date, my mind was constantly at odds with my body. If you believe that your body is like every other Asian's, then one way to stand apart is to make sure that your mind isn't. Looking for love, especially among white people, was an ongoing fight against the fungibility of my Asian body in America. For Asian Americans like me, finding that one person who might be right for you is not only a search for love but a search for individuality. Individuality here is a resource. It's parceled out at birth for white Americans, but it must be earned, at great cost, by people of color, if it ever is. The words "I love you," spoken by someone you believe is the right kind of person, can breathe your life's purpose straight into you.

Like many Asian American kids, I didn't hear my immigrant parents say "I love you" to each other. They knew what the phrase meant and why Westerners used it with each other. It just wasn't for them. In Hong Kong, they had watched Jennifer Jones in yellowface and William Holden in his own face on the beach in *Love Is a Many-Splendored Thing*. The film was released in 1955, a year before the removal of the anti-miscegenation clause in Hollywood's Hays Code, which prohibited the suggestion that real-life interracial romance was desirable. In 1960, my parents got to see Holden with yellow fever again, this time opposite Nancy Kwan in *The World of Suzie Wong*. Both films are set in Hong Kong, and I like to picture my parents sitting chastely in the theater, having the time of their lives. The characters played by Holden represent the possibility of freedom for Han Suyin and Suzie Wong, Chinese women threatened by communism and the colonial sex trade, respectively. These segregation-era romances, along with others, such as the Academy Award–winning *Sayonara* with Marlon Brando, imagined the possibility of interracial heterosexual love as long as the man was white and the woman was Asian but open to becoming less so.

The movies of my generation were no help. Bruce Lee was already gone, and we Asian American boys asked too much of him anyway. I didn't know about his love story with Linda until I saw Jason Scott Lee and Lauren Holly playing them in *Dragon*. In *The Slanted Screen*, Jeff Adachi's documentary on Asian men in Hollywood, the Korean American comedian Bobby Lee reflects upon the only Asian male character everyone in his generation knew. "My nickname was 'Long Duk Dong' in high school because of that character, and I think every Asian guy that ever went to an American school's nickname was 'Long Duk Dong' because of that character," Lee recounts. "That means you're not going to get any girls." Played by Gedde Watanabe, Long Duk Dong appeared in *Sixteen Candles*, a staple even among my students today. Long Duk Dong lusted after white girls and spouted cringey one-liners because he wasn't expected to say "I love you" like the white lead Jake Ryan was. The artist Adrian Tomine captures his complex feelings toward Watanabe in a comic entitled "The Donger and Me." In the cartoon, Tomine watches Watanabe in *Sixteen Candles*, shouting, "You stupid fucking asshole!" at the TV. But after interviewing the actor, Tomine gains respect for his dedication to his career in racist Hollywood. That is, until he watches Watanabe thirteen years later in *Booty Call*. "You stupid fucking asshole!" Tomine shouts at the TV in the last panel.

Wanting to date white people was how I thought to counter the stereotype that Asians all look alike. It wasn't a struggle on behalf of all Asians but just me. When it came to romancing like white men, which I learned from the movies, finding the right way to say "I love you" seemed to be essential. In Chang-rae Lee's novel *Native Speaker*, Korean American protagonist Henry Park, reflecting upon why his white wife may have left him, considers the difficulty the words always presented. There were too many ways to say them, he realizes, and too much room to dissemble when you did: "You could say it in a celebratory sense. For corroboration. In gratitude. To get a point across, to instill guilt in your lover, to defend yourself. You said it after great deliberation, or when you felt reckless. You said it when you meant it and sometimes when you didn't. You somehow always said it when you had to." Our white peers got a head start on this education. For those of us who grew up never hearing our parents say "I love you" to each other or to us, figuring out how to do so ourselves was like learning a secret language, decoding some old WASPy locution on the SAT. It ought to be a core lesson in middle school social studies, immediately following the Bill of Rights. Or in health class, immediately before the condoms. In any event, beginning at that age, I knew that I needed to be fluent.

*　*　*

The eighties didn't have terms like "internalized racism" to explain our Asian American melancholy to us. We didn't even know to call ourselves "Asian American." Color blindness was what you hoped for from your white friends, but it wasn't always possible to avoid the topic of being Chinese. Maybe one of them would audition a racist joke, or another wanted to speculate on who would be valedictorian and why. Your kindest friend might lean over then and tell you that they didn't think about you as Chinese that way, and you could only hope that they meant it when you needed them to. They were saying that I didn't do anything Chinese enough to make them notice that I was. This made sense because I took my lead from them and not from the other Asians at school. Some Asians were like me, assimilated native or one-and-a-half-gen kids, while others had parents who had fled Communist revolutions of their own in Southeast Asia, or were refugees themselves, those I surreptitiously mocked behind their backs. When I was twelve or thirteen, my uncles who dropped by the house would drill me about whether I had any "girlfriends," the number always plural. "I'll bring you a wife back from China," one of them teased, and they would all laugh at my spastic rebuff, which they must have seen coming. Perhaps like Yung Wing, I'm not sure what I hated more: the prospect of a Chinese wife or the implication that I wouldn't have any other kind.

My sister Selma was the only Asian American I trusted when it came to fitting in. She was three years older, and she would drop bits of advice for me like crumbs whenever she had nothing better to do. "If you wear that green shirt, people are going to think you're horny," she said one morning during my freshman year. She had inched up the social hierarchy of our high school—not to the top, which was impossible, but to a respectable upper mid-tier. She joined the drill team and spent Friday nights at football games with other girls decked out in their matching white

western hats and boots. The team was run by a new teacher
—a former Kilgore College Rangerette, I was informed—
who also taught my art class, and one thing my sister and I
had in common was finding ways to impress Miss Jordy. It
surprised us all when Selma started dating. Her boyfriend
was a white guy who drove a white Camaro Berlinetta.
All I remember about his looks was that he had feathered
hair and was shorter than I thought he would be. He was
friendly to me for obvious reasons and even let me drive his
car before I had my license, but he turned out to be cruel
to my sister in ways that she never spoke of. "The Berlinetta
isn't like an IROC," Selma said out of the blue after they
had broken up. "It's a girl's Camaro."

One joke I tell my students every semester to explain
internalized racism is that among my two sisters and me,
we married four white people. When Selma brought my
future brother-in-law home to meet my parents, the first
thing my mother said to him was "Hi, Alan. You're tall. Are
you Catholic?" My little sister Teresa's first husband left
her for reasons I still don't know. Teresa and Mike met in
pharmacy school at the University of Texas and planned to
move in together after graduation. They should go ahead
and get married, my mother said. At Dallas–Fort Worth
International Airport, Teresa came close to discovering her
engagement ring hidden in a piece of luggage. Mike beat

her to it and decided to pop the question then and there. The *Dallas Morning News* ran a story on the proposal with a photo of Mike kneeling in front of Teresa with a baggage carousel in the background. It was supposed to be a feel-good story about young interracial love. I once asked Teresa what it was like being in an interracial marriage, and she said that she didn't think about her relationship that way. "Does Mike think he's Chinese?" I couldn't stop myself from saying. Maybe they divorced because his parents were asking him the same thing. At their wedding, my responsibility was to bring a pair of my pants for Teresa to walk under. "So you'll get married too," my mother explained. It was the most Chinese moment for Teresa and me at any of our weddings.

In *Minor Feelings: An Asian American Reckoning*, Cathy Park Hong discusses what it means to be an Asian woman in this country, "reminded every day that her attractiveness is a perversion." Hong found herself pathologizing her sexuality. "If anyone non-Asian liked me," she writes, "there was something wrong with him." I had thought the Asian girls like my sisters had it easier than me, because most of the Asian women on TV were supposed to be attractive, like Rosalind Chao and Tamlyn Tomita. Growing up, I had the privilege not to have to think about my looks refracting through the cultural noise of Asian female fetishization, which could lead to a violence I didn't have to fear. It was the time of Stanley Kubrick's *Full Metal Jacket*, which gave white men and boys permission to talk pidgin about Asian girls, especially those from Vietnam and Cambodia, but girls like my sisters too. Yet I seemed to have an unspoken agreement with the Asian girls at school. We were never an option for each other. We didn't get into each other's way when it came to dating outside of our race. We did this even doubting that we would go into interracial relationships as equals. If our experiences as girls and boys had anything in common, it was the intermittent suspicion that the white person we were with couldn't possibly want us for who we were, still less for the person that our differences might enable them to be.

* * *

My first girlfriend was a white girl named Marian Olson who had recently moved to Texas from Virginia. She had grown up in Ohio and pronounced "button" with a prodigious glottal stop, which I thought was sexy. She was a tall brunette with an overbite and looked like the actress Jamie Donnelly, who played the Pink Lady Jan in the movie *Grease*. I was a senior, and she was a year behind me, although we were about the same age. We met in Spanish class, which, for a person of color, was as close as you could get to a safe

space in a high school at the time. Having to speak *en español*
made everyone a little less cocky, leveling the playing field.
Maybe that was what gave me the confidence to ask Marian
out. She had just broken up with our school's star thespian,
getting a bad reputation for her trouble. My friends looked
a little worried for me whenever I talked about her. I didn't
care. Marian was smart and attractive and seemed a little
above the gossip about her, which probably wasn't true. If
so, I admired her for trying not to care. She told me that her
favorite place in the world was Montego Bay, which I hadn't
heard of and which made me think that she was worldlier
than I was but also that she could see herself leaving Texas
for good, unlike the rest of us.

My father liked Marian and broke out the hospitality
for her whenever we hung out at the house. I rarely saw him
that gracious, as if he were trying to impress a rich client.
Marian returned his good cheer without any adolescent
awkwardness, really diving into the conversations, I could
tell, because she asked questions. She was more mature
than other girls and knew how to talk to adults. Dad always
pressed a couple of bills into my hand for dinner out. I'm
sure it mattered to him that Marian was white. Maybe he
knew what the stakes were for me. Even though she was
the new one in town, he acted like we were the ones being
judged.

Marian lived in a nice house alone with her father. Her parents were divorced. Her father, the first time I met him, didn't bother to look up when I said hello. The only memory I have of him speaking to me was during a fleeting snowstorm, the kind north Texas saw every few years back then. He was driving me home from their house because the roads were bad. Marian and I sat in the back, silently counting the cars on the side of the road. "A little snow and everyone just loses it here," he complained, shaking his head. He spoke as if we should be embarrassed for being from Texas. His eyes rolled up to the rearview mirror to see if I was listening to him. "You know?" he said.

I let Marian take the lead when it came to fooling around. We usually parked somewhere private, in the lot of a public playground or next to a green space after dark, when there weren't many other people around. One night, a bright light pierced the windshield and swept the interior before we heard the tapping of metal on glass. After I rolled down the window, a white police officer craned his head to get a better look inside. He turned to me, then to Marian. "Everything okay, miss?" he asked. She was flustered but told him that she was all right. He must have believed her. "You know you can't just park here as long as you want," he said to me. He straightened up and walked away after I said we would be leaving. "This is so embarrassing!" Marian said once he was gone, over and over, which surprised me. I had presumed that she had found a way to brush off the judgment of others, but something was different. "I'm so embarrassed!" When Marian and I went out in public on dates, I must have assumed that she was embarrassed to be seen with me as my girlfriend, even though she never once acted that way. I'm sure that I felt she could do better than me for no reason other than my race, which, by design, was not meant to reside solely on my skin but to manifest above and below it too, tainting my tastes and my manners. So when Marian said it out loud, that she was embarrassed, and in a way that implied the fault was mine, she seemed to be certifying the dread that I already knew was there—that not being white meant I would forever be a step behind, proving it by ordering the wrong thing or perhaps reaching for her hand a bit too quickly or eagerly.

But I'm not sure whether Marian was embarrassed about being caught or being caught with me. I wonder if I had been another kind of boyfriend—the star thespian, for one, but almost anybody else who was white—whether Marian would have felt more innocent and less exposed and ashamed that night. But I was as good as invisible to the officer, which was the opposite of what I thought dating Marian would do for me. It also meant that Marian was the only one there to be responsible for her actions. Her embarrassment, most likely, was everything coming together at once: who she thought I was, but also who she thought she was, especially with me, plus the presence of an older white man peering back at her from the front of the car, disappointed. Marian never brought up any girlfriends or her mother, wherever she lived. One time, she mentioned how forward the star thespian had been with her when they were first dating and how, because of her inexperience, it had surprised her, and now I think I may have been the only one who knew that about her at our school, including the star thespian. Maybe Marian thought that *she* was the one being profiled by the cop. What we had in common was a fear of not being individuals, both afraid that how the world looked down on us had to do with our being a dime a dozen in their eyes. Even if I could have explained to her what we had in common, I'm not sure it would have made a difference for us at that time. There comes a point when we can no longer defer, no matter how strong our will, the crush of how we are seen. Sooner or later, we will feel shame for who the powerful and the privileged need us to be.

Marian and I broke up soon after because I kept telling her that I loved her, and she saw that I was serious. Eventually, she pulled me aside and said that she really liked me and enjoyed being with me, but she couldn't say that she loved me and still be telling the truth. She explained this situation to me in the same mature tone I had observed her using with my father and other adults. I didn't know not to say "I love you" or that it was even controversial. It was where you naturally ended up with someone after dating for a while, I figured. At that moment, all the insecurities about my upbringing that I had buried when Marian and I were in public rose to the surface, twisting into a knot of mortification. I comprehended then just how great a leap it took to cross over from dating to love, a lesson that Marian's parents probably imparted to her but mine never gave me or even thought to. Marian and I never spoke again after the end of that year, which was all my doing and a dumb sulk I regret. I came to believe that saying "I love you" sounded different coming out of my mouth, a turn of phrase that wasn't mine and didn't quite translate. Spanish had two verbs for love and was safer.

*   *   *

In May 2014, a twenty-two-year-old college student named Elliot Rodger murdered six people and injured fourteen others in a rampage near the University of California, Santa Barbara, before taking his own life. Rodger's mother was Chinese Malaysian, and his father was white and British. At the time, the reporting of the story didn't refer to Rodger as an Asian American or as mixed race. Yet Rodger obsesses over his race in a 137-page manifesto he released shortly before the massacre. In it, he describes his two Chinese roommates as "utterly repulsive." They were the first two Rodger murdered, stabbed to death along with another Chinese student. But those receiving his deepest scorn were the young, blond white women whose attention he believed he was entitled to. He was ashamed to be a virgin and raged at his perceived inferiors who weren't. "I am beautiful, and I am half white myself," he writes after learning that a Black peer had lost his virginity to a blond woman. "I am descended from British aristocracy. *He* is descended from slaves." Rodger also posted a series of disturbing YouTube videos, including a seven-minute rant entitled "Retribution" shot from inside his car. The sunlight streaming through the passenger window tints the right half of his face a sickly goldenrod as he identifies his intended target, a sorority house and its members who "gave their affection and sex and love to other men but never to me."

A few months later, Christian Rudder, the cofounder of the online dating site OkCupid, published a blog post entitled "Race and Attraction, 2009–2014," a study that tracked OkCupid users' racial preferences across time. In aggregate, the groups drawing the lowest ratings were Black women and Asian men, and little had changed over five years. The study became an origin story of sorts in certain

Asian American circles, revived every so often to explain the plight of Asian American men. In 2015, the Chinese American writer Celeste Ng found herself at the center of a firestorm when she tweeted that she did "not often find Asian men attractive. (They remind me of my cousins.)" Ng, who is married to a white man and has a mixed-race child, was targeted for organized online harassment by a nascent Asian American men's rights movement primed by the OkCupid study. Ng fought back on Twitter and wrote an article for *The Cut*, blasting the culture of harassment against Asian American women who choose not to partner with Asian American men. "About half the women I spoke with shared messages in which harassers called their children (or hypothetical children) 'the next Elliot Rodger,'" Ng reveals. It seemed lost on the harassers, most of them Asian American men, I presume, that their abusive actions brought *them* closer to becoming the next Elliot Rodger.

Rodger is often invoked as the darkest product of the self-hatred Asian American men can harbor about their looks. "It's no mistake . . . that Asian American men and African American women are deemed the least attractive on dating websites like Tinder or OkCupid," said the Japanese American writer David Mura in a 2019 interview. "Asian men are viewed as effeminate, unassertive, and quiet, and all this is attached to our physical appearance." The fear of emasculation has beset Asian American men for as long as I've paid attention as a scholar. State-sponsored oppression played a key role. The 1875 Page Act empowered port officials to ascertain whether "any subject of China, Japan, or any Oriental country" wanting entry into the United States had been contracted for "lewd or immoral purposes." The Page Act was a powerful deterrent to the immigration of Chinese women, and the already imbalanced gender makeup of Chinese communities skewed male even further, to a ratio of twenty-seven men to one woman at the extreme. Eventually, fourteen states banned marriages between whites and Asians. But there are no more Page Acts or anti-miscegenation laws. It can be difficult to determine who or what is at fault for the trouble that Asian American men think they have finding a partner who loves them back. It must have something to do with men believing that they know better than women what is best for them, which was the root of my resentment toward Marian. It's not only the fault of Hollywood and Long Duk Dong. It's not only the fault of residential and occupational segregation. And it's certainly not the fault of Asian American women, whose desires are as socialized by white supremacy as our own, as Mura notes, along with Ng. Ng admits that her tweet revealed "a shortcoming in me, not them, and it's something I've worked—and am still working—to unlearn." Elliot

Rodger assumed that all he had to do to finally be happy was find a blond white girl who loved him back. I doubt it would have mattered to his twisted psychology that the solution was never going to be that simple.

* * *

I met my wife, Robin, in my last year at the University of Texas. By then, my height had peaked at five feet eight inches, and I liked that Robin was as tall as I was, her stature as impressive as her hair, longer and blonder then than it is now. When we started dating, she was still in a relationship with her white boyfriend, who was studying abroad in Germany. After Robin broke up with him, she suggested that we go out on a double date with her best friend, Missy, whom she had known from high school in Amarillo, Texas. Missy had been friends with Robin's old boyfriend, and I was nervous about how I would compare with him in her eyes. The date seemed to go fine, and the next day I asked Robin what Missy thought about us as a couple. "She said that she never thought I would date an Asian man," Robin replied, sounding a little annoyed. Robin let on that the nature of their rivalry at that time had to do with which one might seem more worldly or sophisticated than the other, but I took Missy's remark to mean that my being Asian didn't count as either. At the time, I didn't like it when people defined me by my race, and it seemed as though Missy did just that, insulting and complimenting us both with a single remark. The implication was that Robin was trying to be less prejudiced, which made me "Asian man," not like Englishman but like a Hollywood extra. Even so, I was also flattered that Missy thought that I had overcome whatever handicap my race presented in her eyes. Making that crucial leap from "Asian man" to individual must have been what I was hoping for from a serious relationship with someone like Robin, as if that settled it.

I suspect that there comes a point in any interracial relationship, after a year or even two, when both partners acknowledge, too often in their own minds and ways, that they've outlasted the best that racism had to throw at them. If one partner is white, they may take pride in having assimilated, a bit, to a new culture and endured the sly doubts and questions posed by their own. For me, and for too long, the achievement was to be found in the lasting commitment of my partner in a world full of other options for her, namely those who were white in the one way I couldn't be. With Robin, I feared that if I spoke too much about racism or came across as too angry about it, or if I failed to explain well enough my rudimentary take on what she likely saw as something that was not our business, a Black and white struggle, I would lose her. My solution to this trouble was like a pocket veto. It was safer to be who I was on the double date, the "Asian man" who didn't draw attention to himself as such, especially not one who went on and on about the insecurity or resentment he was repressing. If an interracial relationship leads to marriage, as it did after almost ten years for Robin and me, it can seem like the slate of any lingering doubts about your inferiority is wiped clean by the authority of the state or God, what you had always hoped would be the ultimate power of these institutions to make you whole. In *Turning Japanese: Memoirs of a Sansei*, David Mura recounts a moment when he accused his wife of leaving it to him to fight racism and not taking enough responsibility herself as a white person. "That's ridiculous," she said. "I married you, didn't I?"

The fights Robin and I had were never about my inability to be or do something because I was Chinese, at least not from her perspective. Rather, they spun out of my burgeoning sense of myself as a person of color, jump-started after I left Texas for graduate school. What I was learning was not so much about Asian American grievance as about racial formation, namely about white and Black Americans and what made them so. This meant that I began to see Robin more as a white person than I ever had before, but in a way that didn't automatically cede the advantage to her. I was returning us to the categories of "Asian man" and "white woman" that had organized Missy's imagination but without assenting to its hierarchy this time. For me, it took far longer than a year or two of marriage to feel as though I had outlasted what racism had in store for us, because I began to see it everywhere—in a nonchalant gesture or remark, say, or in the way one of us responded to it or didn't.

But who among us Asians doesn't think that our commitment to the white person we love is different from the rest, or will be, simply because we've made it this far against the odds that maybe only we knew were there? I had proposed to Robin in a hansom cab clacking through Central Park. Only hours earlier we had been atop the North Tower of the World Trade Center, at Windows on the World, toasting our Chinese American friends at their wedding, which would be featured in an episode of the cable TV show *A Wedding Story*. I think we both hoped that our own nuptials would be as grand and as definitive an event. But our wedding day neither demarcated the end of those troubles nor augured a more progressive era as Yung Wing's had done. In fact, joining our lives meant there would be even more time and opportunity for tension.

* * *

After I got married, loving white people meant not talking about racism as much as I would have wanted to—with my wife, yes, but especially with her family. Silence was possible for any number of reasons. For one, my in-laws rarely brought up racism as a topic of discussion. It wasn't obvious to them how Asians could be the victims of it, unless it was at the hands of Black people during the LA riots, and any suspicion they may have harbored that they had it better than my own family because they were white was eclipsed by the exhibit of our marriage itself. Like my parents, they couldn't understand why I might take any more interest in racism against Black people than they would, their own interest being limited to the most egregious violations of civil rights. And they didn't connect how American wars in Asia produced anti-Asian racism at home or follow how I might feel any kinship to other Asians like the Vietnamese. My father-in-law had been a captain in the air force and had flown bombing runs over North Vietnam as a navigator in an F-4E Phantom II. I hadn't raised these concerns with Robin before we married, partly out of my fear of scaring her away but also because I was still making those crucial connections too. When I did raise my concerns, I didn't always speak up. And so another reason not to talk about racism was my own, which I thought was love. Staying silent about Vietnam was like penning a thousand sonnets to my wife. Many years later, my father-in-law admitted that he regretted that part of his service and that Americans had had no business being in the war. In another conversation, I brought up Muhammad Ali, who had also felt a kinship with the Vietnamese, and the only thing my mother-in-law had to say was that he was a draft dodger. I wondered then what it must be like to see such things of this world so differently from your wife or your husband and still never think to part.

Although my in-laws accepted and loved me as one of their own, I rarely fully relaxed over holidays at their home or on vacations on their dime. I sensed that Robin was eager to blend back into the spaces and roles she had occupied as a girl, deferring to the notions of her father and especially her mother once again, a filiality I had long abandoned with my own parents. I felt alone at those times. On any given day, there was just as much chance of my in-laws flaunting their white privilege as there was of them telling me how much they loved me. It can be hard to understand how those who are kind to you can be cruel to others who look just like you. But as the writer Rich Benjamin explains, "One Black man is a delightful dinner guest; fifty Black men is a ghetto." One Asian man must be a son-in-law. You are quite simply outnumbered most of the time, which makes loving you easier. You can even stop seeming Asian or Black to your white family, especially if you enjoy what they do—the same food, the same movies, the same sports teams—because you grew up with these things too. You remind them of themselves, which is always ingratiating. It's only when you don't that all of you remember why you don't. For years, it was hard for Robin to disagree openly with her family because she had grown up with their ethos of calm and consensus, so different from the habit of my own relatives, who fought to find a reason to be mad. Robin eventually began to tell them when they were wrong, which didn't change anyone's mind, except maybe mine. Once, Robin told me, her little sister, Alison, even accused her of blindly parroting my opinions. "You're like his concubine," Alison had said.

When our son Jacob was three, my father-in-law presented him with a framed print of the F-4E Phantom II, handsomely penciled in profile and colored by the artist and captioned "The Fighting Eagles of the 334th TFS." Robin hung it up in the guest room above the bed my in-laws shared when they visited us. The print was an apt token of the white entitlement I regularly steeled myself against when staying with my in-laws, only now this spectre was encroaching upon my own home and the mind of our young son. "I'm not comfortable with that in our house," I confided to Robin. She told me that she understood how I felt but also that she knew the print meant something different to her father—the camaraderie he had shared with his squadron. "It doesn't mean Vietnam to him," she said. The F-4E

Phantom II was a kind of trophy for my father-in-law, I understood. He believed that his time in Vietnam was a grave mistake, but he also believed that it could be detached from the pride he felt for arriving at what he learned was the proper station of a man in this country. I knew what it was like to grant yourself the benefit of the doubt this way. After a brief discussion, Robin and I compromised by agreeing that after her parents went home, we would stash the print in the closet until their next visit.

In time, I learned that not talking about racism to avoid being alone was hedonism or bad faith or both, but not love. In the introduction to the third edition of *White Like Me*, the writer Tim Wise shares some of the reader responses to earlier editions, including one crediting his book with saving a marriage. "I felt pretty good about that until a few months later," Wise writes, "at which point I was told by someone else that my book had helped hasten her divorce." This other person, who was also grateful for the prospect of a better life, realized that her differences with her husband, when it came to thinking about racism, "were too vast to bridge." The institution of racism can topple that of marriage. The longevity of any interracial marriage may not necessarily be a success story. It can signal an evasion of racial differences and not a triumph over them. It's too easy for Asians to accept that our duty is to become more like our white partners, a future that the Qing court feared Yung Wing would bring about but also one that the Connecticut Yankees welcomed as progress. From television and from my white girlfriends and wife, I learned to recite the words "I love you" like the alphabet and to hold hands in public and embrace without pause or qualm. I did not talk enough about racism, even when I knew better, to show my love or hide my insecurities or both. Mine was an arranged marriage too, if not in origin then in purpose, good for keeping the present civilization going.

*　*　*

In 1967, Chief Justice Earl Warren wrote the majority opinion for a unanimous decision in *Loving v. Virginia*, the landmark Supreme Court case that struck down the anti-miscegenation laws in sixteen states, all in the Deep South, including Texas. "Marriage is one of the 'basic civil rights of man,' fundamental to our very existence and survival," he argued. "Under our Constitution, the freedom to marry, or not marry, a person of another race resides with the individual and cannot be infringed by the State." In 2017, in recognition of the case's gold anniversary, the Pew Research Center released a report entitled *Intermarriage in the U.S. 50 Years after* Loving v. Virginia. The report seemed to corroborate the findings from the OkCupid study, this time when it came to marriage. Black men married outside of their race at twice the rate of Black women, while a fifteen-point difference separated the rate of Asian women marrying outside of their race and that of Asian men doing the same. Among Asians, who you married depended a lot on whether you were an immigrant: "Almost half (46%) of U.S.-born Asian newlyweds have a spouse of a different race or ethnicity," reported Pew, the highest rate of any racial group. Over half of all Asian women from this group married outside of their race. There seemed to be less opposition to interracial marriage too; only 9 percent of non-Asian respondents said that they would oppose a relative marrying an Asian person, an eleven-point drop since 2000, the year Robin and I were married.

It might strike us as obscene to quantify an essence as ineffable as love between two people. We want to believe that who we come to love is a fate well beyond our control, which it is, but maybe not in the way we expect. In this country, geography, not chemistry, is the deep structure of love. I have been either an individual or an Asian man depending on where I was, sometimes morphing before the very eyes of those I thought I might love. After Marian, what two of those people saw, luckily for me, were stars. American love isn't the child of the double helix but of the city and the suburbs. It is property taxes. It is a Spanish class paid for by those taxes. The Warren court had it wrong, not in its decision but in its rationale. We fall in love not as individuals but as individuals within groups, those bounded by race but not exclusively. "You're more likely to marry out of your race than your class," my colleague tells his students, most of whom pay the same tuition, just as Robin and I had done when we were in college together. Yung Wing and his fellow CEM students waltzed with the daughters of the Connecticut elite before Yung married one. Maybe my father liked hosting Marian because that was what a house in the suburbs was for, not only to shelter us kids but to send us to good schools with those who might now be our peers. None of this makes the bond that survives such a fixed system any less dear, if I am any example of it.

There are no incantations that you and your partner can whisper to each other to contrive a lasting intimacy, unless, of course, you speak the truth. From a young age, I believed that saying "I love you" to others was the same as showing love to them. This was a misconception. I erred again in hoping that my pained silence about right and wrong was also a sign of love. I wanted love to be a thing to show off to the world, a fetish that could arrest race and class, as if they were not moving targets, ever evading our attempts to banish them. The print of the F4-E Phantom II resides permanently in storage now, even after my father-in-law's passing, there being so many better symbols to remember him by. Loving, more so than love, makes it clear that the relationship is a process, ongoing and evolving, one that takes nothing for granted. It all might be gone in an instant if you are not humble or careful, which is an immigrant's lesson if I ever heard one. Growing up in my parents' house, there was less talking about love and more showing it in your deeds, which is what I had witnessed as a child and should not have forgotten.

CHAPTER 6
MADAME CHU'S

When I was a young boy, my parents briefly entertained the idea of opening a Chinese restaurant. My father had lost his job managing a fabric shop in Long Beach only a year after taking us out of Hong Kong in 1971. I was not even three years old. He may have started cold-calling storefronts again, the way that he had landed his first position, but he was probably thinking bigger by then. He looked into buying a McDonald's franchise but neither had nor could borrow the six-figure stake. ("They didn't want to sell to Chinese," he concluded, much later in life.) Then there was the possibility of a life outside of California. When the unemployment ran out, Dad put the four of us in the VW Bug and drove us to Texas, closer to family. His two younger brothers were going to school near Dallas, and his cousin Michael wanted to partner in a business there. Our family moved into an apartment complex in north Dallas called, inauspiciously, Lazy Acres, yet it was there that my father and Uncle Michael sat down to promise their industry to each other. Maybe they envisioned a high-class franchise like Trader Vic's, the fabled birthplace of the mai tai, where my mother had waitressed. In the end, however, as my mother tells it, my father and Uncle Michael looked at each other and admitted, each in their own way, that they didn't know how to cook, and that was the end of that.

I grew up thinking any Chinese person could open a restaurant. I think my father would have liked running one at first. In the seventies, he was probably still a little flattered that Americans liked Chinese food as well as they did. It was how the comity between any two peoples must naturally begin. I remember one of his oldest friends from his days in Hong Kong, a white man from California whom I called Uncle Owen, raving about my mother's cooking. "Violet, your restaurant should be called Madame Chu's," he told her. Uncle Owen could have been the reason my father at first confused American affection for Chinese food with American affection for us. Nixon's visit to the People's Republic of China seemed to put things on the right track. "We didn't understand what discrimination was when we first got here," my mother said. "We didn't expect people to discriminate against us." Uncle Michael had opened a Chinese gift shop called Flower Drum in a north Dallas shopping center. Maybe he was thinking that there was nothing more American than a Rodgers and Hammerstein production like *Flower Drum Song*, a story that seemed to promise him that he would now belong. Its most memorable number was "Chop Suey," sung in the 1961 film adaptation by Juanita Hall, who was not Chinese but Black. Uncle Michael's shop went out of business before too long.

It was just as well that my father didn't open a restaurant. Running one would have made it harder for him to exceed his customers' expectations of him as a Chinese person and as an immigrant, even if the well-meaning among them didn't know enough to admit it. He wasn't suited for the hospitality industry, beginning with the assumption that he should be there to attend to the needs of his customers, which he might not have abided even if he had been getting rich. But then there would come the inevitable judgment of him and his talents. The issue wouldn't only be a question of whether diners gave their compliments at the end of their meal or whether they returned for another one the following day or week. It would also be how the arrangement made comparing him with other Chinese people seem not only natural to his customers but also proper. He put up with enough white customers pointing out that his prices or selection of goods was worse than those of the other Chinese vendors. I suppose he got tired of being the model of the model minority. Yet he grew to be more like these customers than he probably imagined, suspicious of any newcomers with something to share, which he saw only as something to prove. I think he wanted them to know their place.

It seemed that my father truly enjoyed his food only when we kids were enjoying ours. Whenever we went out to eat, he confirmed that we were happy with our choices before turning his attention to his own. Restaurants were stressful places because so much was liable to go wrong: the wait for a table, which one we got, how long it took to get our food, how hard it was to flag down the server when that food wasn't right, and so on. But when everything went smoothly, which wasn't terribly often, my father went home in a great mood, proud, as if the universe had momentarily righted itself for him. For this reason, he didn't like to try new places and almost always ordered the same dish at the few that he came to trust. I realized that he and I saw dining out in this country quite differently. For him, it was not a treat but a kind of necessary trial, one that he had to outlast to meet his responsibilities to others, mostly to us and our families, with the hosts, cooks, and servers—even other guests—playing the antagonists. He was ready to take oversights personally, every missed refill or undercooked steak a reminder that he wasn't getting what he thought others were. But his vigilance was primarily on our behalf, I know now, as if we were dupes or marks and didn't know what we were truly deserving of.

After I left Texas, I noticed that my father didn't seem to enjoy Chinese food once he began to think about it as such. He approached Chinese-run restaurants with the same hesitation that he brought to the anonymous American grills and cafés that sprung up in the suburban retail hubs near our house, except that his behavior was more outspoken and entitled. He could be gracious and generous if he knew the owner, whom he then expected to greet us personally and to check in on us during the meal. Other restaurateurs were suspect by default, especially recent immigrants. He eyed the dishes with the same skepticism he held for the server who spoke no English. After a while, he stopped ordering the authentic, ornate dishes meant for the whole table to share, the mu shu and pancakes he grew up with and the fried flounder that he had encouraged us kids to eat because it was "brain food." The last Chinese restaurant he trusted was in Atlanta, and after he was forced to close his office and showroom there, how he ordered elsewhere became more guarded and less imaginative. Toward the end of his life, he expected us to order for him in good English, our true and meager Chinese American filiality. He wanted his own steaming bowl of wonton soup noodles minus the dumplings and swirled an inky stream of soy sauce into it before hunkering down to take a bite.

*   *   *

Asian food, like Asian people, is never not probationary in this country. Keeping that association alive is also a way of keeping Asian people in their place. In 1969, the New York City Health Department sent orders to Chinese restaurants in the city to limit their use of monosodium glutamate (MSG). It was investigating the so-called Chinese restaurant syndrome that led diners to complain of unpleasant symptoms after eating Chinese food. According to the *New York Times*, epidemiologists "found that a teaspoonful and even tablespoonful were being added routinely to wonton soup in some restaurants." In the journal *Social History of Medicine*, the historian Ian Mosby argues that the national obsession with MSG reflected long-standing xenophobic and racist attitudes toward the Chinese. Despite its widespread use in other ethnic cuisines and manufactured food, MSG was an issue for Chinese food only. Even my father quizzed our Chinese servers about their kitchen's use of it, despite its presence in the fast food and corn chips he gobbled down while on the road. Restaurants advertised in storefront windows and on menus that they used "No MSG." Researchers found that respondents were much more likely to associate negative symptoms with eating out when asked specifically about Chinese food. These ranged from "tightness," "burning," and "numbness" all the way to "depression" and "detachment." Any malady of the digestive or nervous system could be blamed on Chinese food if you stopped to think about it.

But the most objectionable ingredients purported to be in Chinese cuisine were not man-made. Nineteenth-century American periodicals and advertisements circulated the familiar image of a Chinese man dangling a giant rat by its tail above his gaping jaws, ready to make a meal of it. In 1883, the *New York Times* ran a story headlined MOTT-STREET CHINAMEN ANGRY. THEY DENY THAT THEY EAT RATS—CHUNG KEE THREATENS A SLANDER SUIT. The story begins with interviews of the European neighbors of "Chung Kee, whose real name is Mr. Wong," who claim that the "Chinamen" next door had been preparing rats and cats in their kitchen. Yet when the district's sanitary inspector visited the residence, along with a reporter, both found "nothing suggestive of rats or cats about the place." Wong Chin Foo, the civil rights activist, journalist, and publisher of the *Chinese-American* newspaper, offered a $500 reward to anyone who could prove that the Chinese ate cats or rats. Wong said that he "had never heard the rat story until he came to America. There was no necessity for the Chinese to eat such food here, he said, as they were all making money." An astute observer of the purpose of white supremacy in America, Wong might have guessed that it was the making money that was objectionable, not the rats and cats.

In 2001, the Pulitzer Prize–winning political cartoonist Pat Oliphant went back to this well of stereotype to comment on an international crisis between the United States and China. An American spy plane had collided with a Chinese fighter jet near Hainan Island, resulting in the presumed death of a Chinese pilot and the detention by China of twenty-four American crew members until the United States issued a formal apology for entering Chinese airspace. (The crew initially complained about being served fish heads, a local dish of the island community.) Oliphant, whom the *New York Times* called "the most influential editorial cartoonist" in 1990, depicted Uncle Sam at a Chinese restaurant about to be served "crispy fried cat gizzards" by a bespectacled, bucktoothed Chinese waiter who resembled then Chinese president Jiang Zemin. The waiter trips and spills the gizzards on Uncle Sam, then stamps his feet and demands an apology. The Asian American Journalists Association criticized the cartoon and called on Oliphant to stop using racial stereotypes in his work. The cartoonist Gene Luen Yang parodied Oliphant in *American Born Chinese*, the first graphic novel to be nominated for a National Book Award. Yang's grotesque caricature Chin-Kee offers to share his lunch of cat gizzards and noodles with his cousin, both students at "Oliphant High School." There is Chinese food and then there is Chinese food, apparently. Yang calls out

Oliphant's racist assumption that like Chinese food, Chinese people also have an essential core that will always be foreign and revolting to the West. Oliphant was reminding Jiang Zemin to know his place.

To non-Asians, what makes us Asian is not the rice or noodles but the pets on our plates, or at least the possibility of them. In 2021, the comedian Jay Leno apologized for a career of telling jokes about Asian people eating dogs. The apology followed a fifteen-year campaign waged by the Media Action Network for Asian Americans against Leno, who told a dog-eating joke as recently as 2019 on *America's Got Talent* in a scene that was later scrubbed. Leno explained that he "was making fun of our enemy North Korea, and like most jokes, there was a ring of truth to them." Yet Leno also admitted that "in my heart I knew it was wrong." Continuing to do what you know is wrong is also continuing to know who has the power to hold you accountable. About a week later, in Texas, the Carrollton–Farmers Branch Independent School District suspended three teachers for a multiple-choice quiz question about "Chinese NORMS." It asked middle school students whether it was normal in China "to cut off someone's lips if they burp in a restaurant," "to give children fifty lashes by a cane if they steal a piece of candy," or, in parts of the country, "to eat cats and dogs." The school is in my hometown and where my sister Teresa went, about a mile and a half from the house we grew up in.

White Americans who ask Asian Americans if they've ever eaten dogmeat are trying, at some level, to find out how far they're allowed to go in the relationship. Those who have asked me that question may have done so out of an inkling of curiosity about its taste, but their primary motivation was frankly to have one over on me, which they did, no matter how I answered. It's the same with anyone who tells a dog-eating joke around a person they perceive as Asian. They mean to recalibrate their standing with that person—just in case the roles were getting too ambiguous for their liking. Leno used the "ring of truth" excuse to suggest that he's not the only one to blame, but for what, he doesn't say. Just as American English doesn't boast a truly cutting epithet for all white people, popular conceptions of white American foodways are likewise rigged in favor of the dominant culture. That is, there is no domestic dish so awful that eating it dehumanizes its eater, at least not one that can't first be associated with Black people or poor white people or their distant European ancestors. Your food is all a twelve-year-old middle schooler needs to know about you, because nothing else matters about your culture after its people are willing to eat that. There's no talking your way out of it with barbs of your own, no tit-for-tat comparisons with exotic American fare, because, despite what we all know about its ingredients, a hot dog is still not a dog.

In America, talk about dog eating is a drawn-out slur. It is never literally about dog eating but about the dog eater, which I learned from Jessica Hagedorn's 1990 novel, *Dogeaters*. The book follows the lives of a diverse group of Filipinos across a tumultuous three-decade period ending in the mid-eighties. Hagedorn said that she wanted to reclaim the word from its purported origin as a slur used by American soldiers during the Philippine-American War. Her editor did not like the title, and many Filipinos "were upset" about it, she recounts, mostly because of a sense of cultural shame. Hagedorn "had intended it as a metaphor." That war, which started in 1899, was the first war in Asia fought by the United States. "Gook" started there too. Perhaps the prosecution of all the wars in Asia to follow was justified in the minds of Americans because of dogmeat. A dog gave you its unconditional love and instantly forgave you for the sins you were capable of. Not eating dogmeat is a metaphor as well, for the fullness of your humanity. "Dogeater" is not only a metaphor for a people but also for their relationship and history with another people. For those who invented the word and would brandish it now, it is a statement about love, more specifically about their capacity to embody it more than anyone else.

*   *   *

The nexus of the perpetual foreigner and the model minority stereotypes of Asian Americans must certainly be the Chinese or Asian restaurant in this country. It is there that the dissonance generated by these dueling meanings of us is regularly put on display. The movement linking Chinese restaurants and moral and social decay became organized in the last decade of the nineteenth century and lasted for about thirty years, according to the legal scholars Gabriel Chin and John Ormonde in their article "The War against Chinese Restaurants." Chin and Ormonde explain how labor unions largely orchestrated legal actions that sought to ruin the Chinese restaurant industry by arguing that it was a threat to white labor as well as to white women. They cite a 1902 essay by the then president of the American Federation of Labor, Samuel Gompers, "Meat vs. Rice: American Manhood against Asiatic Coolieism—Which Shall Survive?," which laments that Chinese laborers can subsist more cheaply than their white counterparts. In 1909, the sensationalized murder of Elsie Sigel, a young white missionary, by Leon Ling, a Chinese restaurant worker, drove home the assertion that Chinese restaurants were merely fronts for vice, such as opium dens targeting white women for sexual slavery. White activists boycotted Chinese restaurants and endorsed laws that targeted Chinese businesses by denying them operating licenses and even the option of hiring white women to work there.

The proliferation of Chinese restaurants in the early twentieth century was due not to some ancient Chinese talent for cooking, as I had thought as a kid, but to dominant stereotypes of Chinese people—spread by exclusionists like Gompers—that kept racist and xenophobic legislation in place. The Chinese restaurant explosion was not about culture and ethnicity but about social status and race. The Chinese Exclusion Act of 1882 had barred most Chinese immigrants from entry into the United States, but it included an exception for merchants and their families. The historian Heather Lee researched how a legal challenge resulted in Chinese restaurant owners being admitted into this class in 1915. The bar for entry was high, however; Chinese restaurants needed to be "high grade" establishments ("*chop suey* palaces," explains Lee) and be managed by a single person only who was not allowed to perform any menial labor—like waiting tables or washing dishes—for at least a year. Yet Chinese immigrants discovered a workaround, Lee found, and "pooled their resources and opened up restaurants as partnerships." Investors took turns in the managerial role for a year at a time, thereby earning merchant status, and eventually were able to reunite with their families still in China. In New York, the number of Chinese restaurants quadrupled between 1910 and 1920, "and then more than doubled again over the next ten years," Lee says.

By the time Chinese exclusion officially ended in 1943, Chinese restaurants were seen as less threatening by white Americans because the same could at last be said for Chinese people. Less than a year before, *San Francisco Life* published a photo of the Chinese American Charlie Low at Forbidden City, his upscale restaurant and nightclub that inspired *Flower Drum Song*. Low is sandwiched between a smiling Ronald Reagan and Jane Wyman. The most popular memoir written by a Chinese American was *Fifth Chinese Daughter*, a coming-of-age story about the author, Jade Snow Wong, but told in the third person. Published in 1950, it introduced her version of immigrant Chinese culture to a curious white readership during the period between the exclusion era and the rise of the model minority stereotype. "Jade Snow," as Wong refers to herself in her book, is constructed as the prototype of the model minority. *Fifth Chinese Daughter* was translated into eight languages, and the State Department sponsored Wong on a promotional tour through Asia during the Cold War. Multiple chapters invite readers into Chinese restaurants, including one scene in which the Wong family entertains Jade Snow's white professors from Mills College. Earlier, Jade Snow had discovered that the surest route to acceptance by her professors and peers was to cook a Chinese meal for them, commensality apparently being the answer to xenophobia. The book even includes instructions for preparing an authentic tomato beef dish. In the seventies, the Chinese American writer Frank Chin argued that the only two forms of writing that Chinese could publish in this country were the autobiography and the cookbook. Chin was being hyperbolic but made his point. Both forms required us to explain ourselves in terms that white Americans could understand, since recipes for success were still recipes.

Perhaps no other piece of popular culture better illustrates the vacillation between "good" and "bad" stereotypes of the Chinese restaurateur than the 1983 film *A Christmas Story*. By 1997, the film had become so popular over the holiday season that one network aired it continuously for twenty-four hours between Christmas Eve and Christmas Day. It chronicles the misadventures of a white boy named Ralphie Parker growing up in Indiana in the 1940s. At the conclusion, the Parkers' Christmas dinner is ruined by a pack of neighborhood dogs who invade the house and devour the turkey. Mr. Parker takes the family to Chop Suey Palace Co., where they are the only diners. The Chinese staffers serenade them with carols but have trouble with "Deck the Halls" and "Jingle Bells," predictably transposing the "l" and "r" sounds. When a roast duck—head and all—is brought out as the main course, Mrs. Parker loses what's left of her composure, shrieking after the head waiter produces a cleaver and decapitates it tableside. The scene is supposed to be as absurd as all the family antics that have preceded it, Chinese food and hospitality absurd in and of themselves. Yet the experience is remembered fondly by Ralphie, the year that they "were introduced to Chinese turkey." In 2017, Fox aired a three-hour-long special entitled *A Christmas Story Live!* that diversified the cast and included a Filipino American quintet nailing "Deck the Halls" without an accent. It got bad reviews.

The original *A Christmas Story* captures the prevailing meaning of Chinese food in this country perfectly, I think, whether it is 1943 or 1983 or 2023. As an option, Chinese food is always there, even on Christmas and in the smallest towns, but the expectation going in is that it is never quite ideal, either too salty, too oily, or just plain bad for you. It's a setup for a punch line, about how the name of a dish is pronounced or what might be found in it, sometimes both. As teenagers, my friends and I caught Eddie Murphy's stand-up special *Delirious* whenever it aired on HBO. It debuted the same year as *A Christmas Story*. "Everybody makes fun of the Chinese when they order some food up and shit," Murphy starts his bit, pretending to be a customer mocking a Chinese cook's accent. He squints and bares his front teeth. The audience roars. But Murphy's cook gets his revenge in the kitchen. "Yes, very funny. Very funny.

Make a special wonton soup for him," Murphy singsongs, pretending to cup his penis while thrusting. This line kills even more, just as it did in our living rooms, and for the rest of the night I would repeat it for my friends to get them to laugh, a kind of double yellowface. I liked the bit because Murphy made the Chinese guy know what was up, unlike the hapless Chop Suey Palace Co. staff, the joke ultimately being on his racist customer, but I also knew that people were still laughing at the accent and the eyes and the teeth. And the sneakiness too. Even so, Murphy made being Chinese seem a little better, if only because he chose to mock white people too, an option I hadn't previously thought was on the table.

*   *   *

Before my father retired, his favorite restaurant was the Rendezvous in Memphis, a touristy rib joint off a downtown alley in the shadow of the Peabody hotel. Over his years of traveling, he had gotten to know some of the waiters, older Black men in bow ties and starched white shirts who never quit, he said, because they made so much in tips. "Hundred thousand," he whispered to me, having probably come right out and asked them at one point ("How much you make?"). There was always a line of customers out the door and down the alley, but we walked right past it and into the restaurant.

Once he found a waiter he knew by name, we were seated almost immediately—my father palming him a twenty for his trouble—jumping the line of Beale Street tourists. He could eat at least two racks of the dry rub ribs, along with the sides, and he would order another rack for me before I was done with the first. I think he liked that there was really only one item to order and everyone knew it, that it came out fast and delicious, and that the staff treated him like an old friend. The hanging sign in the alley claimed that the restaurant had opened in 1948, which made me wonder whether we would have been allowed to eat with the white diners fifty years earlier. We may have had to come in through a different entrance to sit in a different room, or been allowed to order takeout only, or not been allowed to enter at all, let alone cut in front of white people. Or maybe our dinner would have played out largely the same way. We would have been recently unexcluded, after all, and it would be another year before Mao shook things up again for Chinese Americans by creating the People's Republic of China.

When I think about what restaurants have meant to my family, the nature of this country's deep social anxiety over race becomes clearer to me. So does the connection between anti-Black racism and anti-Asian racism, their common denominator being a white supremacy that must subjugate people of color in public spaces, either with the sanction of the law or without it. Like schools, restaurants are powerful, visible sites of social equality, which is why labor unions sought to wipe out chop suey joints during the exclusion era and why white racists ignored and harassed and beat civil rights activists sitting at lunch counters in the 1960s. As the historian Grace Elizabeth Hale suggests in *Making Whiteness: The Culture of Segregation in the South, 1890–1940*, racial segregation in southern public spaces was more of an idea than a reality. Black people and white people found themselves in proximity to each other all the time, even if the roles were server and diner. It was even possible that one of our waiters at the Rendezvous had worked there in 1963, the year before the legal end of Jim Crow. The goal of segregation wasn't to keep groups apart but to establish, unmistakably, the difference in status between them.

The racist faults assigned to Chinese food and restaurants had been anticipated by the familiar tropes associated with Black American foodways. Whether the stereotype was a loss of self-control in the presence of certain foods or a pandemonium of filthy ingredients or conditions, Black Americans knew how foodways could be weaponized to dehumanize them. They also knew better, I suppose. In the South, for centuries, in restaurants and private homes, Black hands cooked and served the food eagerly devoured by white people. In other words, the objections to Black foodways were never really about the food. They were about what the food and the way it was eaten might say about the state of the relationship between Black and white people. At mealtime, what was objectionable to too many, and not only in the segregated South, was the person next to you and not the plate in front of you. The default mode when discussing foodways in the United States is to understand what ethnicity (less often race) has to do with the practices of a group of color. We tend to pay less attention to the foodways of the dominant race, unless we belong to a group peeking in from the margins of it.

Many years ago, I had the opportunity to speak on a panel at the International Civil Rights Center and Museum in Greensboro, North Carolina, and I looked forward to seeing the re-creation of the Woolworth's lunch counter where students from North Carolina A&T started that city's sit-in movement in 1960. I could picture the photo of four students on the second day of their protest, still waiting to be served. But it's another famous photo of the movement from 1963 that stands out most clearly in my mind. The activists Anne Moody, who is Black, and Joan Trumpauer and John Hunter Gray, who are white, sit at a Woolworth's counter in Jackson, Mississippi. Their bodies are covered in sugar, ketchup, and mustard; one young white man is in the act of pouring sugar down the back of Trumpauer's neck. A leering mob of white men swells behind them. Gray later recalled how they pulled Moody's and Trumpauer's hair and hit him with brass knuckles, cut him with broken glass, and burned him with cigarettes. "There was a good deal of blood," he said. These acts of violence too are foodways. They are not much older than some of my mother's American cookbooks. In the history of the United States, group culture has never been static but has adapted to the reality born out of the struggle to clarify what it means to be white.

Anne Moody must have known this truth her whole life; Joan Trumpauer and John Hunter Gray learned it in time to do what was right. The morality of a culture is to be found in how we eat, not what.

*　*　*

Group foodways don't begin and end in restaurants. Some of the books and TV shows I consumed growing up made it seem normal for American parents to send their kids to their rooms without dinner. It probably never occurred to mine to punish us by withholding a meal. You're still supposed to laugh at grainy home videos of a little white girl, for instance, her jaws set and arms crossed, in front of a plate of peas, the only person left at the table. It surprised me that these parents, even with all the power in the family, would turn food into a trial only because they didn't observe enough gratitude for putting it on the table.

Several years ago, during the week before Thanksgiving, one of my students mentioned how much she dreaded the holiday dinner with her family. Others nodded knowingly. This discussion spontaneously bursts forth in my classes almost every year now. They are usually white, these students, and their politics stray from or even controvert those of their loved ones. They believe that Black lives matter and that pronouns do too, stances they do not hesitate to defend on campus. It's only when seated at the dinner table with their relatives, they tell me, that they lose their confidence, more often their patience, and, in the worst cases, decide they can't go on and abruptly excuse themselves from the table. Before then, however, the meal begins innocuously. An uncle tells a joke about dining hall fare intended to make everyone appreciate the good food before them now. But the jokes don't stop there, and finally he brings up someone only to punch down on them. The fathers and grandfathers —it is usually men, it seems—take their cue to hold forth like cable TV pundits, the captive audience at the table too much of a temptation. Pushing buttons passes for tough love nowadays. I do not tell my students that we Chinese never scold our children at New Year's. Something dark has crept into the culture, I think, when sparring with your own is an accepted ritual of the national holiday. Except now the young are the disciplinarians, sending themselves to their rooms without dinner to teach a lesson.

Despite its origins, Thanksgiving is a holiday that makes sense to most Asian Americans and, I suppose, to immigrants in general. You take time out to honor those who had something to do with your being alive and together, no matter where you came from. After I got married and before I became a father, I spent every other Thanksgiving with my parents in the house where I grew up. One year, one of us kids suggested that we go around the table to say what we were grateful for—a practice we likely picked up at our in-laws'—but it didn't feel right, as if we knew we were trying too hard to be people we weren't. Our litanies could sound too much like bragging anyway, and we were still Chinese enough to know that nobody needed the kind of fate tempted by that. My mother said the proper Catholic prayer taught to her by the nuns in Hong Kong, which sufficed. Looking back, I'm glad that we didn't compel ourselves to talk when we sat down to dinner, even on Thanksgiving. What made us a family was the eating, not the talking. There were no conditions for being at the table. Eventually, one by one, we popped up from our seats and left without asking permission, usually a grandkid first but perhaps even my father, whose duty had ended with the turkey carving. Most of us kids were gone after a half hour, our white spouses the only ones left, lingering to chat over glasses of wine that the rest of us had raised only to toast.

Our Thanksgiving dinner was a cultural hybrid in ways other than the food. We left ourselves little time to argue with one another, at least at the table. Maybe Thanksgiving should be celebrated by new immigrants only, like the Pilgrims before they decided to take over, a holiday for those happy just to see another year with a bit more in reserve than the last. Instead, it's become an occasion for sharing grievance as much as gratitude, a day to reflect upon what you have as well as what you believe others shouldn't. The peeved might learn something from immigrants, who know how it feels to lose their children to a strange culture too. My parents, for instance, like those of my students, knew about their children coming home from school a little less like themselves every day. About our new words that they didn't understand but were expected to. How we could seem deferential but still act as though they were the ones needing to change. My parents didn't fight us kids on this because they knew that we couldn't be like them and still succeed in this country. Even so, they might tell their white counterparts to have a little grace, on this day especially. Whatever threat exists to your way of life emerges not from our tastes but your own, which, as any immigrant knows, have always savored gratitude without complaint.

*   *   *

In time, my parents' attitudes about feeding themselves and others began to diverge. My mother organized our wedding reception in Hong Kong, the biggest Chinese meal of my life. It would be only the second time I returned there after I left as a baby. My father, by now, had developed anxiety about international travel. "You don't have to come, it's no big deal," I said, loving him by letting him eat by himself, far away from anyone he would have to talk to. "I'll watch the business," he volunteered. My mother's side was almost all the family we had left in Hong Kong anyway. The reception was held in a banquet room at a big restaurant in the Central District. The silk wedding guest book, which our guests signed with Sharpies, had our names embroidered in a vertical column, mine in Chinese above the letters R-O-B-I-N, stacked one atop the other. The waiters brought out course after course, but the only two I remember were the shark fin soup and the roast baby pig. It was an unfamiliar feeling to eat these foods outside the context of race in the United States. Eating the first used to mean that you were a part of something special, although it can signify cruelty now. The baby pig came out looking like it had been flattened

211

into two dimensions, precut into pieces like a jigsaw puzzle. Every table got one, and each guest took a piece. (I asked my mother what it symbolized. "That the bride is a virgin," she said. "Just eat a little bit if you don't like it.") The Chinese do not have a monopoly on commensality, especially at celebrations—Robin's family had thrown the first reception for us a week before atop the tallest building in Amarillo, Texas—but a family-style meal with people who were practically strangers was an experience I hadn't had since I was a boy, when I couldn't choose to avoid such things.

Getting married finally let me see my mother truly enjoy her food for once. At meals, Mom always took the bad parts of a dish for herself: the gristly chicken leg, the bruised and ugly grapes. The rest of us let her do that. When my father was out of town, she cooked American food for my sisters and me and ate leftovers herself, even the rice, saving the fresh pot of it for us. She would then eat from that pot the next day. She probably learned this process from her own mother. When I worry about her as the only one left in the house now, I like to imagine that at least she has no choice but to claim the prize morsels from the dinners she makes for herself. But my guess is that she doesn't do so right away, stashing them in the fridge for later, perhaps for days, helping herself only when it seems like no one else would want them.

My father's diet, on the other hand, steadily became more solitary because of the nature of his job. He seemed to prefer to eat on the go, or at least as quickly as possible, as if food were meant only to end a person's hunger. In this one way, at least, ours was the only country for him. As kids, we learned that the sandwich to get from McDonald's was the Quarter Pounder with Cheese, never the Big Mac, whose goofy proportions must have struck him as a bridge too far, its special sauce too exotic to risk. When we traveled for work together and stopped for fast food, he pulled the cube van right up to the drive-through window, costing us only twenty minutes or so on our trip to or from a show. From the passenger seat, I observed him plumbing waxy boxes from KFC or Church's or even truck stops to pull out a drumstick or biscuit. He folded slices of New York–style pizza in half and wolfed them down like John Travolta in *Saturday Night Fever*. He sat down for dinners mostly for my sake, I knew, and even then I managed to ruin one of the few relatively guiltless items he enjoyed. At a chain restaurant in some suburban mall, I made conversation by mentioning how I still enjoyed a Caesar salad even though the dressing included raw egg. Dad stopped mid-chew and frowned as if the kitchen and I had played a prank on him. To my knowledge, it was the last Caesar salad he ate.

There were many points at which I might say that my father's mind became Americanized, but his body no doubt arrived at that point in 2002, when he was diagnosed with type 2 diabetes. He was a year shy of seventy, and his age had finally factored into the etiology. Up to then, his nonstop labor seemed to counter the effects of his diet, but even that couldn't outpace time and bad choices. It was hard for him to limit the rice and noodles he still ate at home, the only things he could be expected to like. At first he was good about counting carbs and testing his blood. Home for Christmas, I might scold him for sneaking an extra peppermint stick, the soft kind that he could suck on because he had lost most of his teeth. I think I expected him to manage his urges with some innate asceticism I had long ago ascribed to him. After one dinner, my sisters and I were ostentatiously gorging ourselves on some confection now off-limits to him. "How can you eat that in front of me?" he snapped. It was the only time he ever hinted that he should have as much as we did, an ugly assimilation accelerated by the diabetes. It was one thing to watch your kids take first dibs because you wanted to and another because you had to. When we still thought he would go home from the hospital after his stroke, my mother told me that his happiest moment was when he was handed an orange-flavored Popsicle, which he bolted like a banana.

Food is the language of love but also of insecurity, perhaps because the two are forever tangled. When I was away at school, my parents would tell me to go out to eat using their credit card, which I later learned they were not paying off every month. Maybe it was their way of balancing one worry with another. Their satisfaction when we all sat down to eat together, I found, flowed out of their peace of mind about our welfare, as tangible as any embrace. They almost never let me do the same for them—buy a meal for them, that is—my mother sneaking away from the table like an assassin to take care of the bill while I was chatting with someone or just glancing away. The worry eventually reverses its course in a lifetime, but I have had little success assuaging it, just like my parents. As with trying to discipline your child with food, you can't tell your parents what to eat or not eat and still expect everyone to walk away with their dignity. It was pointless to offer either advice or money, both gestures an insult for all to recover from. I had to learn to not see the Quarter Pounders and packs of cheap ramen that my father was putting into his body in his last couple of years. The Chinese greet you by asking you whether you have eaten rice. Saying that you have is the same as saying "I'm well." When I try to answer the question of why I wasn't with my father when he died, I remember how easy it was to stop asking him about his dinner only because I didn't want to hear him tell me what was in it.

*　*　*

At the start of the COVID-19 era, one might have supposed that white Americans did not worry about their elders or else did not want to. It might have been a cultural thing. In April 2021, the popular podcaster Joe Rogan told his millions of listeners that he would advise twenty-one-year-olds not to get the vaccine, to trust in their youthful immune systems instead. About a year earlier, Dan Patrick, the lieutenant governor of Texas, a septuagenarian himself, argued that American grandparents should be willing to risk their safety to keep the nation's economy on track and off lockdown. The Gen Z spring breakers and Gen X frequent flyers should be allowed to carry on. Patrick knew that older people were more likely to die from COVID-19, even if he didn't know by how much (eight out of ten deaths, according to the CDC). Later that year, a story by Olga Khazan in the *Atlantic* cited a study called the "Moral Machine experiment," in which participants had to choose between killing different groups of people. "Overall, older men and women were some of the *least* likely to be spared, ranking just above dogs, human criminals, and cats," Khazan reported. "People like dogs," concluded Azim Shariff, one of the authors of the study.

The psychologist Susan Fiske found that "the only American cultures that have consistently positive views of the elderly are African Americans and Native Americans." How did Asian Americans miss the cut? The common denominator, Fiske suspected, was a younger generation appreciative of the wisdom gained through a lifetime of adversity.

Yet COVID-19 did bring Asian American generations closer, in more ways than one. The era was full of possible culprits to blame for the forced lockdowns and mask mandates, none more prominent than Asians. As a vector, food seemed like an obvious way to connect Asian people to the contagion. It was easy because the suspicion was already there—of filth, duplicity, or just plain funny business. A ramen restaurant in Texas was vandalized with racist graffiti on its exterior windows and tables: NO MASK, KUNG FLU, COMMIE, HOPE U DIE, RAMEN NOODLE FLU, GO BACK 2 CHINA. The week before, its Vietnamese American owner had appeared on CNN and criticized Texas governor Greg Abbott for lifting the state's mask mandate amid the coronavirus pandemic. The owner received death threats and resorted to carrying a gun for protection. In California, the Chinese American owner of a family-run butcher shop was forced to hire a security guard after a series of confrontations and acts of aggression, including a customer caught on camera leaving a mutilated cat in the business's parking lot. When the owner shared the incident on social media, some users blamed the business itself for butchering cats and dogs. These crimes are part of an ongoing rash of racist violence targeting Asians in the United States that took off during the pandemic, which also precipitated an economic downturn that disproportionately hurt Asian-owned small businesses. But as in centuries past, the racists did not fear for their health so much as for their status.

The real threat we posed to the racists wasn't that we carried the coronavirus but that we cared about it. In their eyes, the chief transgression of these Asian entrepreneurs, and of all Asians in the country protecting ourselves against it, really, was that we put our self-interest above theirs in public. It was a novel foodway. We cared about our lives. We cared about them so much, and about those of our loved ones and coworkers who looked like us, that we dared to do what few expected us to, which was to tell those we didn't know they must do in our presence. We cared enough to tell them to wear a mask and to keep their distance when they leaned in too close for our liking. They were the unknown, the compromised, not us. It wasn't their judgment to pass on the worthiness of the food or service any longer but ours to pass on their worthiness to have them. In our restaurants and nail salons and spas, they had to do what we told them, just like everyone else in the place, or they had to go. It must have been foreign and unexpected for them to feel this way, especially around us. We were the ones who were supposed to serve them, after all, even on Christmas. Our rules must have felt like segregation. But we trusted our own because we knew none of us could ever take our safety for granted. It was as if we knew something about the racists that they did not—their Jim Crow and sit-in sins—that told us in no uncertain terms that we were the ones imperiled.

* * *

There will be no recipes here. No author's step-by-step account of a Chinese dish or life has ever made the rest of us appear any less inscrutable to strangers. The credit always goes to the one doing the cooking or the reading anyway. Perhaps Charlie Low, Jade Snow Wong, and my father and Uncle Michael were mistaken. Introducing Chinese food to this country may have made things worse, on the whole, for Chinese people. Chinese food is too easy to find and too inexpensive when you find it. It's not like French or Italian, which can call itself fine dining without much argument, but more like Mexican—popular enough, as long as it knows its place. A food's status depends on whether the people who cook it are still immigrating. Chinese food doesn't even stay Chinese in America. The Asians and Latinos staffing the kitchens of Panda Express or P.F. Chang's are just following orders, concocting the glazed standbys dreamed up by American appetites. It was how American Chinatowns invented chop suey in the late nineteenth century. In *The Search for General Tso*, the filmmaker Ian Cheney asks native Shanghainese to identify a photo of American-style General Tso's chicken. None recognize it. "It doesn't look like chicken," says one woman. "It looks like frog." The real General Tso, Zuo Zongtang, was a Chinese patriot who resisted Western imperialism during the Qing dynasty, says the writer Jennifer 8. Lee. American Chinese food has always been the comfort food of those who have colonized it, its take-out menu the story of no one else's lives but their own.

But my sisters and I made American food our own too. When we started public school, my mother began to supplement the Cantonese and Shandong cuisine she made for herself and my father with the postwar American standards whose recipes she usually got off the side of a box. All of us might begin with a bowl of bitter watercress soup, but then we kids would dig into the ground beef casseroles or Shake 'n Bake pork chops that my parents never touched. A side of white rice with everything, even cheesy au gratin potatoes. Double starch. In my parents' eyes, the more we ate, the better. If we didn't care for the main course, we ate mostly rice and soy sauce. If we couldn't finish what was on our plate, my mother would glance over at it and tell us to "eat the meat," a reasonable compromise still. My father ate like an American in a more fundamental way, which is to say that he ate like an individual, accustomed to individual packaging and individual portions and individual tastes. He was the only person I knew who ordered his Quarter Pounder cooked "well done," which used to embarrass me but seems quintessentially Chinese American now, I think, merging his Old World tastes with assembly-line gratification.

In America, it was hard for us to eat like a Chinese family for very long. My father was on the road for months out of the year, the dinner table quieter and tidier without him, but not in a way that any of us liked. How he earned a living made us kids more American but our mealtimes less traditional. The big family meals were always going to dwindle as we kids grew up and left the house one by one until it was just my parents left. But there must have been a time, maybe in the seventies when we were all still small, when we thought that our meals together might go on forever, growing more ambitious even, my mother's range diversifying with every new entrée sampled in school cafeterias and family restaurants, all those wonderful lasagnas and barbecued briskets. When I go back to the house to visit, we eat off the same set of dishes in the cabinet from forty years ago, the same microwave-safe floral stoneware that my mother collected a piece or two at a time from the Safeway, discounted if you bought a week's groceries. Heirlooms now. The old house is still my favorite place to eat when I return for my annual visit, my sisters and their families dropping by because I'm there but also because Mom will be cooking.

I asked my mother how my father was eating before the end. She said that on most nights his dinner was a bowl of rice and a dish of salty bean curd. "To be honest, I'm a bad cook," she added. I hoped that Uncle Owen wasn't just being nice. "I never tried to make anything new except for you kids because I knew your father wouldn't touch it."

"I always liked what you made for us," I replied. "Dad was a picky eater."

The saying goes that we Americans order too much Chinese food because we're not used to sharing. I haven't seen a lazy Susan at any kind of restaurant except Chinese. We do not seem to eat together even when we eat together, every diner a sovereign at a state dinner. Families feast to celebrate getting out of the house and not a return to it. This is the culture worth solving in these times, not the inscrutable civilization of the Orientals, who have eaten together for many thousands of years and probably will for thousands more to come, to the dismay of the spray painters and rock throwers and shovers of the elderly. Americans worry too much about the origin of what we put into ourselves and not enough about the origin of what is already there.

CHAPTER 7
PAPER SON

I n high school, I was recruited for the Academic Decathlon team because of my reading skills. I had developed a reputation as a strong student in English/language arts, which basically meant that I was good at reading literature and writing essays about it. Academic Decathlon was essentially a national standardized test-taking tournament that covered subjects such as fine arts, economics, and math, as well as language arts and essay. The national champion was as close to a teenage polymath as you could find in those days—a regular on the morning-show circuit—but most of us excelled in only one or two subjects. The best team won $5,000 scholarships and the attention of elite colleges. Our team wore matching wool sweaters (the brand on the label was Game Day) with a torch and laurel tastefully embroidered over the left breast. We had coaches. Mrs. Smith was a soft-spoken white woman with red hair and a sweet Texas accent who invited our team to study at her home on weekends, assisted by her daughter, who was our age and also had red hair. The other coach was Mr. Jump, a short, blond white man who was younger than Mrs. Smith and more profuse in his passions, which made sense because he tutored us in music and art, introducing us to the nuances of jazz and Jackson Pollock. Both prepared us for the language arts and essay portions of the competition by helping us to read the assigned novel, which for two years in a row was about Africa. In my first year on the team, it was *Cry, the Beloved Country*. The next year it was *Heart of Darkness*.

That was the year our team made it past the regional meet and into the state tournament outside of Houston. The school to beat was Pearce High School in Richardson, Texas, which had fielded the last three national championship teams. Our principal, Dr. Blanton, a husky white man who resembled the actor Joe Don Baker, scheduled a school-wide awards ceremony and pep rally for our team. We were told to wear our sweaters and the medals we had won at regionals, unmistakable from a distance dangling from the red, white, and blue ribbons around our necks. The nine of us stood in a row while the varsity cheerleading squad ran out to perform specialized chants, which I don't remember a single word of, only that they had been tailored to encourage us to demolish our opponents with our minds. More than a thousand students watched us fidget from every angle. Our team was diverse, at least by the standards of the day. Three of us were Asian American, and one teammate was Black, a girl named Stephanie. In the yearbook photo of us from that day, most are looking at the ground for some reason, but my eyes are locked on Dr. Blanton, who is enthusiastically pointing an index finger at me as if we were in the middle of a game of charades.

At practice we approached *Heart of Darkness* like any other subject—that is, like a body of knowledge to take in and process as the occasion required. I chased it with CliffsNotes, which I must have bought on my own. The characters and plot we knew by rote, but a good reading meant yoking elements to the themes, which back then warned of the depravity that might overcome anyone— meaning Kurtz—who allowed things to get out of hand. We drilled each other in what an image or bit of dialogue "meant," as if Joseph Conrad or his book were solely in control of that process. (On a shelf in my bedroom in my parents' house, I rediscovered a sheet of theme paper with crib notes penned in my high school cursive: "jungle— barbarism—dark part of man" and "Marlow—detective of the conscious.") The answer to each multiple-choice question snapped in like another piece of the puzzle. Mr. Jump wheeled in an AV cart for watching *Apocalypse Now* on VHS (sans permission slips) to show that what endured about the story were the themes, the jungles of central Africa and Southeast Asia interchangeable in their purpose. Eventually our team coalesced around a singular reading of the book, one that may have been a little better or worse than that acquired by the tens of thousands of other smart kids across the country that year, but, at its core, like theirs, held that a descent into savagery was incremental and an equal-opportunity situation.

Looking back, I suspect that the novel selection had something to do with the divestment campaigns and boycotts directed against South Africa at the time, in full swing and implacable, the reports of which inevitably crossed our dinner table like everyone else's. Apartheid was the kind of social problem that the Academic Decathlon prepared future leaders to address. I didn't know Stephanie as well as I knew the others, and I wonder now what she may have been thinking while reading *Heart of Darkness*. Perhaps it was something like what I felt screening *Apocalypse Now*, which was a kind of self-enforced detachment from feeling. I may even have been taking notes on that story too. I shifted into that state of mind whenever I had to see a story through. I know now that the detachment can be the first step of the learning process but must not be the last. But detachment governed everyone else's reading too, except maybe Stephanie's, grooved by these tales of white people in South Africa or the Congo or Cambodia—anywhere but here. Nobody in them was anybody we knew. Stephanie was not the Africans, we Asians were not the Montagnard, and the others were not the white imperialists who had lost themselves away from home. Reading books became an activity as detached as solving for x. If we had any relationship with our books, if our reading had anything at all to do with us, it was about our future, about how our talent for reading would justify our place in the wider world, and certainly not about our past, which we understood only in terms of our personal lives, so tender as to be measured out by grade level.

Our school didn't win at state, nor did we place or show, although we took home a silver medal in a team event. I didn't win an individual gold medal for my reading as I had hoped, but my Korean American teammate did for her essay. Jeanie was our ringer, the smartest one on our team. She was no stranger to competition, a brown belt in tae kwon do. Her younger brother was even better, a black belt from a young age. I didn't know him but had heard the stories. One was that he practiced on campus by kicking a tree branch above his head. His name was Eugene, and I assume that at some point he was bullied for that on top of for being Asian. He was small for his age, dwarfed by the beefier, half-shirted cowboy wannabes we called "ropers." Another story—it could have culminated the tree story or been a different one—was that a group of older students were bent on bothering Eugene, perhaps mistaking him for Vietnamese, and Eugene told them, politely, I heard, to leave him alone or they would be sorry. They didn't stop, and, as the story goes, he let them have it.

*   *   *

In the eighties, it wasn't especially controversial for a consortium of public high schools to require its students to read a book explicitly about racism and then reward them for parroting back a canned, predetermined take on it. Before too long, however, such a curriculum would then be denounced as a kind of indoctrination, but indoctrination to what, exactly, depended on the era. Students were thought to be threatened by the ideas of a conspiratorial "Cultural Marxism" in the nineties and aughts and by those of "critical race theory" (CRT) now. I assume that *Cry, the Beloved Country* and *Heart of Darkness* managed to dodge the onslaught of "parental challenges" and state lawmaker scrutiny because the anti-Black racism in question wasn't homegrown but of seemingly European origin and an ocean away besides. Today, the books that endeavor to say something about American racism are the ones that become targets for removal from libraries and school reading lists. According to the American Library Association, some of the most challenged books of

2020 included *Stamped: Racism, Antiracism, and You*, by Ibram X. Kendi and Jason Reynolds; *The Bluest Eye*, by Toni Morrison; and *The Hate U Give*, by Angie Thomas. These books share an understanding that anti-Black racism in the United States is an ongoing reality. Yet the list also included *To Kill a Mockingbird*, by Harper Lee, and *Of Mice and Men*, by John Steinbeck, both of which include anti-Black racial slurs that, presumably, were deemed to be bad in and of themselves regardless of context. The act of reading about racism now is a panicked hunt for words and plots that would threaten to turn you into a racist or else reveal you to be one.

Although not as prominently as Black writers, Asian American writers have also been targeted in the movement to censor or ban books about racism. In 2020, the Central York School Board in Pennsylvania imposed a classroom "freeze" on dozens of anti-racist books, videos, and other resources assembled after the murder of George Floyd. It included the Mindy Kim series, by Lyla Lee; *The Name Jar*, by Yangsook Choi; and *A Big Mooncake for Little Star*, by Grace Lin, among others. Student activists won a reversal of the ban a year later. A month after that, days before the start of Banned Books Week, the author Kelly Yang learned that her debut middle-grade novel, *Front Desk*, had been banned by the Plainedge School District in New York. The novel is based on Yang's experiences as a young immigrant from China who helps her parents manage a motel. One chapter includes an incident where a white police officer falsely accuses a Black character of theft, a scene that made *Front Desk*, in the eyes of a concerned parent, a "CRT book." The well-organized campaign against CRT (or whatever idea might be attacked in its name) objects to school curricula suggesting that racism has been a structural constant in this nation's history and is built into social institutions such as law enforcement. On its website, the group No Left Turn in Education even includes a parent's letter complaining about *Front Desk* as an example of how to advocate for its position on "parental rights" in education. I wondered when this latest book-banning movement—usually grassroots in appearance but often funded by wealthy conservative donors—would begin to implicate Asian Americans. At the time Yang tweeted about her book being banned, I was preparing to ask my students to read and think about how racism is portrayed in Celeste Ng's novel *Little Fires Everywhere*.

When I was part of the Academic Decathlon and was reading novels about racism only to answer questions about them, I never imagined that I might end up doing it for a living or would even want to. When it comes to the subject of racism, I've found that Americans tend to be bad readers, white Americans especially but not exclusively. This doesn't mean that they don't comprehend the book's material but that they don't question it, at least not in a self-reflexive way. This, ironically, is also the fear of those activist parents who get angry about a young adult book's portrayal of the police or of gay or transgender characters. They believe that their children will unwittingly accept whatever meanings the book presents to them. Each one of us, except perhaps when we were very young, when meanings were more fluid, probably has been or still is a bad reader in this sense. While we may question the craft or message of a book, outside of sacred texts, we usually do not think to question our relationship to it, or at least not the way we would second-guess ourselves after quarreling with an old friend. But maybe all books are sacred texts because they should be for learning about ourselves. "Book! you lie there; the fact is, you books must know your places. You'll do to give us the bare words and facts, but we come in to supply the thoughts," said Stubb, who was only second mate on the *Pequod* but coined a first-rate idea. *Moby-Dick* was the longest book I ever asked my students to read. Those who couldn't finish usually said that it was too thick, or too boring, or too grim, or too much like the Bible, all reasonable conclusions. All I asked was for them to admit it was they, like the legions before them, who made it so. In the same way, I was a bad reader for much of my life, even as I believed, and was reminded, in one way or another, that I was a proper disciple.

*   *   *

My mother said I was five years old when I learned how to read. Every few weeks, she drove me to Richardson—the suburb that would produce the powerhouse Academic Decathlon teams—to check out books from the closest public library to our apartment in Dallas. Most of the books in our home in those days came from there. Mom somehow talked the elementary school into letting me skip kindergarten and enroll directly into the first grade when I was five. "They let you do it if your preschool teacher said you were ready," she explained. She had had trouble learning English in grade school in Hong Kong and was held back twice because of it. In 1961, she immigrated with my father's sister to Seattle to get her diploma from Edison Technical School and by then was fluent, a late bloomer. Because I was born in October, she probably thought that it was better to get me in early rather than late so that my teachers would goggle at my precocity and not my simplicity. She was right. In the fifth grade, a teacher named Mr. Clodfelter, a white man with a thick mustache who always wore a suit to school, went out of his way to find my mother at parents' night. He was smiling at her when he held up an index finger and told me that the Chinese believed that their babies, when they were born, were already one year old.

At mealtimes, when my mother told one of us kids to "set the table," she meant that we should take some newspaper stacked on the chair no one ever sat in and spread it out across the oak dining table like a tablecloth before arranging the place settings. When it was my turn, I used the classified ads because it was the least valuable section, but when my sisters did it, they didn't seem to care. None of us ever used the Sunday comics, which would have been extravagant. We didn't talk much at dinner, which was about eating the soups and stir-fry my mother had made, messy foods that splashed or plunked down onto the newspaper amid clumps of rice. If I was bored, I rested my head on a palm and read the stories from the *Dallas Morning News*, some of which were a few days old because we weren't allowed to use that day's paper. "Clearing the table" meant putting all the dishes into the sink and then disposing of the newspaper by folding it up from the edges as if wrapping a present in the middle of the table. Mom then wiped down the table with a wet rag. My elbows were a dusty gray from rubbing on the ink, but I also absorbed enough about current events to impress my teachers. Most of the time, I read only the first parts of some stories and began others in the middle, a few turned upside down or sideways.

My good grades convinced many people, beginning with my teachers, that I was a strong reader. I wasn't like most of my Asian classmates, non-native speakers of English, who people assumed were bad readers because of their remedial tracking and thick accents. Reading badly was an unspoken expectation for immigrants in Texas, as unremarkable as bilingual street signs, which meant that whatever proficiency I demonstrated was flattering for everyone involved. I must have called to mind those Asians who win the National Spelling Bee, whose talent seems enough like reading at first, but by the end of the tournament reminds people of the kid who can recite the first few hundred digits of pi. It wasn't hard for me to be a good reader in this basic sense. The great abolitionist Frederick Douglass tricked white boys into teaching him letters, a serious crime in his day. Douglass was a true reading prodigy, not because of how he learned to read but because of how he read.

In time, the quantity of every American's reading will seem more impressive than the quality of it. Most people believe that after a certain age you end up reading the same way as the person next to you, our chance to show off ending with the SAT. Reading is literacy once again, nothing special, as much like problem-solving as driving a car to the store once you learn how. It is not about making decisions but the opposite, which is putting your faith in the judgments of others. It is easy to imagine Asians, especially immigrants, sitting at attention, eyes forward, as if seated in a row of students' desks. We're here to listen and not to question or, worse still, digress. For despite how difficult telling stories about ourselves should be, white Americans love to do it. The secret to being tolerated, if not welcomed, among them, if that is what you want, is simple. All that is required of you, all that has ever been required of you, is to like the same stories they do and to let them tell you why they are good.

*　*　*

American children get off on the wrong foot when reading about racism in school. Even at its best, a textbook makes it difficult to question your relationship to it because the dynamic is too one-sided, like that between a stern lecturer and his pupils. I grew up in Texas when the Texas State Board of Education was at the peak of its influence over textbook selection, before updated curriculum standards, school district autonomy, and technological advances phased out a system that could promote a single text for national adoption among tens of millions of students. In 1982, the year I was in seventh grade, *Texas Monthly* profiled Mel and Norma Gabler, the founders of Educational Research Analysts (ERA) in Longview, Texas, a modest operation that exercised outsize influence over the shape and content of the national curriculum. ERA was dedicated to scrutinizing prospective textbook copy and organizing conservative activists to lobby against the "secular humanism" creeping into the curriculum. They objected to a book that "cited both Martin Luther and Martin Luther King, Jr., as reformers," noting that "Martin Luther was a religiously dedicated, non-violent man." Describing America as a "nation of immigrant[s]," according to the Gablers, presented "a derogatory view that did not foster patriotism." For most of my time in the Texas public schools, it was this shining idea of patriotism that overshadowed the racism in the stories I was told, the way a minute hand will predictably cross over its partner.

As a kid, I loved war stories, which, after a certain point in history, are also stories about racism. Those that captivated me the most were the stories about underdog Americans who lost in the beginning only to win in the end. My father let me stay up late with him whenever the networks aired his favorite movies, like *Tora! Tora! Tora!* or *Patton*. It was easy to root against the Japanese, but I was confused that the Americans called Erwin Rommel a genius even though he lost and was a Nazi. I discovered that enslaving Black people, like fighting for Hitler, also did not stand in the way of being admired if you died for a cause that was not slavery, which I suppose Rommel had going for him too. In the seventh grade, we were required to take Texas history, where we learned about all the wars that had happened in our state. Our textbook, *Texas: The Land and Its People*, had a burnt-orange cover and was the thickest of all the books I had to bring home. It was easier for me to understand the stories from that tome than those, like "The Scarlet Ibis," from our literature reader. For the Texas history fair, I proposed to my friend Brad that we build a scale model of the Battle of the Alamo, where the greatest Texans had made their stand—Davy Crockett a celebrity even in his day—even though they had also lost.

Brad and I spent our afternoons and weekends leading up to the history fair working on the model. The base was a sheet of plywood big enough to board up a window. I bugged my father to drive me to the craft store for other supplies. The aisle of model train miniatures dazzled me—tiny storefronts and billboards, a universe of anachronistic Americana fantasies. My father balked at the price of the foam crumbles that looked like grass ("Why not use grass?") but paid for them anyway. To fashion the adobe walls, I smeared Elmer's School Glue onto strips of corrugated cardboard and dipped them into plates of sand, like I was breading fish filets. I felt a duty to get each detail just right. Brad and I arranged dozens of plastic toy soldiers with care, General Santa Anna's Mexican troops, painted blue, out-numbering the beige Texans by almost ten to one. Brad and his father sometimes referred to Mexicans as "wetbacks" in front of me as if I knew what it meant, which I didn't at first, other than it was bad. Some words you had to hear instead of read to know the true meaning. I hoped that others would see from our model that the Texans were cunning and strategic, the Mexicans dumb and overconfident.

Our project was supposed to present Texas history in a way that people didn't already know. Most thought that the mission's chapel was the entire Alamo. "The Alamo is the whole thing," I said. The first time I visited it, I didn't expect to see it only a block away from grubby drugstores and parking lots. We were right that people at the fair mistook the chapel for the Alamo itself, but we didn't have the whole story either. Our toy marksmen could not have taken cover behind the iconic parapet, which was added years later. Not all the Texans had fought valiantly. The desperate tied white socks to their bayonets and tested their Spanish ("¡Tengan clemencia, valiente mexicanos!"), while deserters were cut down by the lancers waiting for them. Davy Crockett, who went by David and was from Tennessee, was probably captured and executed. Santa Anna had ordered no quarter, but he spared women, children, and enslaved Black men. Our textbook did not say that slavery was illegal in Mexico and was why the Texans did not want to be Mexicans anymore. Spanish-speaking Tejanos also fell at the hands of Spanish-speaking Mexicans. And the Texans had parleyed with the Cherokee and their allies to protect their northern frontier. Brad and I had painted only beige and blue figures.

We were told that "Remember the Alamo!" was about remembering those who had died for liberty, a sacrifice Brad and I thought we were commemorating. But the liberty at stake at the Alamo seemed always to belong only to white men like its commanders, William Travis, who owned slaves, and Jim Bowie, who trafficked them. Over time, it must have been easier to remember the losing than the slavery, even though the Texans put the latter in writing. The 1836 Constitution of the Republic of Texas barred "Africans, the descendants of Africans, and Indians" from citizenship, and Black people could be neither free nor emancipated in Texas. None of this appeared in our textbook. "Remember the Alamo!" sounded like you were being told to pay attention to history, but it was the opposite. Those who said it made you think that they remembered more than you did or could. You were to skip ahead. As a boy, I didn't know that the Texans could not be beige without others being blue, or Black, or Indian. They were beige precisely because they weren't Black and blue. Our model, which froze time, should have reminded us. But we read about the battle only after its conclusion, which settled things.

Our project won a ribbon but not the purple one for the grand prize. Brad and I then had to decide who was going to keep the model. I'm sure that our respective parents rooted for the other kid, because it was useless now, massive and fragile at the same time. We decided to cut cards for it, which seemed like the mature solution. I lost. For a while, I saw the model in Brad's room whenever I dropped by, but we hardly mentioned it and tossed the football or played computer games instead. One day it was just gone. Maybe Brad had struck a deal with his parents that gave them permission to get rid of it. At the end of the year, I won the Texas history award at our junior high school. Texas history wasn't as challenging as other subjects because all you had to do was remember what was already in *Texas: The Land and Its People*. We weren't allowed to write in the book, only our names on the front pastedown. Reading was just remembering the names of generals and rivers. The fair was the only time you had to apply your learning, and then all you were doing was embellishing a story already told. I got a fancy blue foil certificate with my name written in gold paint, which my parents put in a metal frame from the craft store and hung on the wall, next to the photos of our relatives.

* * *

Several years ago, rummaging through our attic, I came across a box of mass-market paperbacks from my days as an undergraduate. Among them was a copy of *The Bluest Eye* I didn't quite remember, the one with the photograph on the cover of a Black girl and white doll. The book turned out not to be mine at all but belonged to my wife, who must have read it in a general education course before we met. I decided to peek at her annotations. Her script had not changed much over the years, and in the same attractive hand that I came to know, I saw the words "white view" written in pen next to the first paragraph. I wrote nothing of the sort in my books in those days. I was familiar with "point of view," which was when the narrator either knew why everything happened or didn't depending on the designs of the author, who apparently always knew. It occurred to me at that moment—I was over forty—that other students back then were reading Toni Morrison when I wasn't, and this fact, on top of the evidence before me of how that was happening, induced a sharp pang of regret about my time in college and the poor choices that I had made.

The only course I took as an undergraduate that included Black writers was an elective called something like "The American South in Literature," and in addition to William Faulkner, Flannery O'Connor, and Walker Percy, we also read Zora Neale Hurston and Alice Walker. It was taught by a white man, a graduate student from West Germany, then in its last year of existence, who spoke with an accent but whose English was better than all of ours. I was surprised that he had come to this country to study these writers, but at one point he suggested that southern writing was the only kind of American literature worth reading for a foreigner like himself. Early in the semester, I caught up with him after class to ask about *Uncle Tom's Cabin*, a book I was liking very much. I don't recall my exact words, only that I betrayed an assumption, painfully, that its author, Harriet Beecher Stowe, was Black. I had even read the biographical introduction, which did not mention her race. "You know the author was white?" he said, no doubt surprised at how bad a reader I was. I must have thought that only Black people would choose to write a book about racism. I was a foreigner too, technically, but my misreading had more to do with my time in *this* country, which was all but a year of my life.

It would have helped me to hear Toni Morrison at Harvard that year. In her lecture "Playing in the Dark," she described how writers such as Willa Cather and Ernest Hemingway drew from fictions of Blackness for the iconic stories that went on to define a national literature. Morrison knew that the meaning of what was in front of her depended on what wasn't. It may be how all virtuosos see the world. Before they were great writers, artists like Morrison were great readers. The first Black woman editor at Random House, she worked with most of the Black writers in the catalog, some her own discoveries, like Gayl Jones, Toni Cade Bambara, and Henry Dumas. In the six years after she left, Random House published more than five hundred titles—but only two, including *Beloved*, by Black writers. The problem was not bad writers but bad readers. It was important not to cater to these readers, Morrison told a crowd at Portland State University in 1975. There exists a "prison that is erected when one spends one's life fighting phantoms, concentrating on myths, and explaining over and over to the conqueror your language, your lifestyle, your history, your habits. And you don't have to do it anymore. You can go ahead and talk straight to me," she said, promising to be the reader her audience needed.

I was in graduate school when I finally took a class solely on Black writers. The reading list comprised over a dozen books of postwar Black writing, and the only author to rate multiple titles, five or six, was James Baldwin. I wondered if the other students were reading everything that was assigned to us, in this class and in others, and I may have finished only *The Fire Next Time* and *Giovanni's Room*. Our class met at night, in late fall in Ann Arbor, and what I remember most fondly about it was our professor putting out a simple tea service for us before we began. His name was Marlon Ross, and he was the first Black teacher I ever had. He was a young professor, a Romanticist by training, who finished off some of his comments with a low chuckle that revealed a gap between his two front teeth like Baldwin's. It was how he looked one night when he said he suspected that his department had asked him to teach the course only because he was Black. I was thinking that it was also my job in the class to discuss what was happening to the Black people in the books we were reading. I chose not to write on Baldwin for the term paper because his novels didn't always make it easy to do that, which turned out to be the point. And besides, in his essays, Baldwin seemed to be more interested in writing about what was happening to white people.

Reading for this class was an exercise in self-consciousness. The class was large for the graduate program, eighteen students, three or four of whom were Black. I was mindful of my reading, but I was even more so of my speaking, afraid of blurting out an offensive notion during discussion. I was conditioned to be anxious about how white people would receive whatever I had to say, but this was a new kind of double consciousness. Blackness shorted the gap between white and Asian. I took longer to share my thoughts, a circumspection that descended upon the others too. We tended to walk back our own claims ("but I don't know"), adding our own nervous chuckles. It was hard to say what we meant because we were also thinking about who we were or wanted to be at that moment. How we read revealed who we had become, whether we knew it or not. The books were our private Rorschach tests. Instead of questioning them, I began to question my relationship to them. More than anything, I felt accountable for my reading—to Marlon Ross, first off, and to my Black classmates, and even to the others who may have read Toni Morrison already or had a Black professor before. But it was something new to be accountable to myself for my own judgments while reading, even to be aware of those judgments in the first place, especially before I got to the end of the book and believed I knew everything.

Reading a book can be confused with finishing it. My best friend in high school, a white kid with a kind face shot through with freckles, started to refer to others as being "well-read," a term I'd never heard before but liked because saying it made you seem smart too. He had finished *The Autobiography of Malcolm X* and told me how Malcolm had believed that white people were devils but by the end of his life realized that they were not devils. My friend seemed relieved to be able to gloss over the prospect of being a devil. Being well-read is not just about getting to the end of a quota of books. Like college-bound students today, my friend had somehow made the book accountable to him with what Baldwin would call the "presumption of his innocence." Students are too often taught to make books about racism accountable to them, asked to find something that they relate to, anything, as if that is their right as innocents. There is nothing special about finishing a book, even *Moby-Dick*. (Jacques Derrida was once asked if he had read all the books in his library. "Three or four," he replied. "But I read those four really, really well.") Plenty of books were half-baked anyway, as Baldwin and Morrison knew, either because there was no one like you in them or because there were stereotypes who were supposed to be like you. Rather than confront the reality they had created, Baldwin observed, white Americans instead chose to tell stories to be able to live with themselves. This "forced Americans into rationalizations so fantastic that they approached the pathological," he wrote in "Stranger in the Village." He called out the vast holes in logic in their stories because they were nothing more than myths, good only for inventing a people or studying one.

I want to say the same about myself, that I was wise to these rationalizations of innocence, carving through them as Baldwin had as a child. After all, for as long as we have been in this country, Asians have been mistaken as perpetual strangers to it, as scabs or else spies, which is bound to bring some clarity among us, if not resentment. Most of the time, however, I was shown sundry kindnesses, not in spite of being a stranger but because of it. Perhaps I was the kind of stranger the country had been waiting for, a post-Hart-Celler tabula rasa. It took me ages to appreciate Baldwin, after all, who despised *Uncle Tom's Cabin*, the first book he ever read. He outed those who could not tell the truth about themselves, which meant that they could never tell the truth about others. A gay man, Baldwin faced censorship of all sorts in his day, but the Central York School District saw fit to ban him too, posthumously, "freezing" Raoul Peck's documentary about his writing, *I Am Not Your Negro*. Baldwin believed that writing was a moral act. Reading is a moral act too. Both have to tell the truth. It was the lie of innocence that my teachers should have told me to read for, as Morrison and Baldwin did, not the assonance or the consonance, which only had you nodding your head in time to another's breath.

* * *

A literature professor is, at heart, a reading teacher. Teaching reading in college, especially teaching reading about racism, requires academic expertise like teaching chemistry, psychology, or any other discipline. But the teaching of reading usually does not receive the same level of respect or resources as other disciplines, because of tight budgets and the belief that being literate and well-intentioned are the only qualifications for the job. In 2019, a video circulated on Twitter showing a group of students at Georgia Southern University burning a pile of books in what appears to be an outdoor barbecue grill next to a residence hall. They were copies of *Make Your Home among Strangers*, a novel by Jennine Capó Crucet, a Cuban American writer and an English professor at the University of Nebraska. Georgia Southern put the novel on a recommended reading list for students in its first-year experience program and invited Crucet to campus for a reading and talk. According to *USA Today*, during a contentious Q&A session with some white students, Crucet "challenged students at Georgia Southern University to think about their whiteness." Later that evening, a student captured video of copies of Crucet's book going up in flames. A university official stated that the book burning was not in line with Georgia Southern's values but defended the students' right to free expression. In a piece I wrote for *Inside Higher Ed* shortly after the incident, I noted that the organizers of the first-year experience program bore some responsibility for the fateful disconnect between what Crucet meant by "whiteness" and what some students took it to mean. The program wasn't prepared to have its students talk about racism because it put the onus of learning on the book itself and, as I discovered later from a faculty member at Georgia Southern, on a crew of earnest but underpaid and underqualified educators. Bad readings also bedevil citywide "big read" events that count on good intentions to make up for knowledge and the skill to deliver it. Colleges and universities too often underfund their obligations to producing knowledge about racism, with predictable and, increasingly, revanchist consequences.

What the book burners and parental challengers refuse to understand about anti-racist curriculum is its effect on their liberty. From their perspective, these books (and, presumably, the teachers who assign them) restrict their liberty by eliminating choices that they believed they once had—namely, to say what they want about others and to feel what they want about themselves, especially if they are white. In April 2022, Florida Governor Ron DeSantis signed into law a bill dubbed the "Stop WOKE Act." Among other restrictions, the law prohibits public schools and private businesses from offering any curriculum that implies that someone must bear "personal responsibility for and must feel guilt, anguish, or other forms of psychological distress because of actions, in which the person played no part, committed in the past by other members of the same race, color, national origin, or sex." Other anti-CRT measures echo this position even though the pedagogy they describe is not one that I have ever heard any serious educator endorse. But these opinions on the value of reading about racism are not limited to off-campus Republican caucuses and parent groups; they also originate from within the institution dedicated to academic freedom and the pursuit of knowledge.

Once, an administrator at my university accused me, in the privacy of his office, of trying to make white students feel guilty for being white. He was an older white man with a square jaw who swept his thin gray hair back away from his forehead, accentuating its prominence and making him look a lot like George C. Scott in his prime. I was his official adviser on diversity matters, on course reassignment from my faculty position, another example of how universities like Georgia Southern and my own address such obligations on the cheap. He had just read a report I had written on the disappointing state of one of our efforts and was angry. I'm not sure where he got that idea about my pedagogy causing anguish for white students, because if he had bothered to review my student evaluations, he would have found that almost none implied such a thing while nearly all were positive, some effusive. I invited him to watch me teach and see for himself, which he never did. He gathered that I sold my white students short and that I took some perverse pleasure in turning the tables on the privileged. Although he later apologized, I don't believe that he ever understood that my white students valued the learning they got from reading about racism for an obvious reason: self-interest. The knowledge they gained in class gave them more choices for how to live their lives, which is the premise for the pursuit of higher education whether you are a first-generation college student or a fourth. This, ultimately, is the outcome that national anti-CRT organizers fear, not that young people will have to endure "psychological distress" or hurt feelings but that they will see the new options for living that segregation has kept at the margins of their consciousness. The fear is not of anti-racist education eroding choices but of it proliferating them, choices that will be exercised on the job or on the streets or at the ballot box.

I think often about a graduate student I had years ago, mostly because she apologized for being a bad reader. Jane was a white woman in her late forties, older than I was, and she had come back to school to write a novel. Our small master's program served mostly locals and near-locals who could attend class only at night—high school teachers eyeing a promotion, recent graduates dipping a toe, serial workshoppers. The course was called Critical Reading, Writing, and Thinking, and we instructors defined those words however we wanted. Like Marlon Ross, I toted an electric kettle and a tray of teas and cocoa with me to our night class. Jane was usually quiet during our discussions of Asian American literature and criticism. She didn't read like her classmates, who were a generation younger and knew to look for the ways that race or gender mattered in a book or in their lives. (Obama would win a second term that semester.) One day Jane dropped by my office to discuss her trouble in class. She began by apologizing, because she wasn't used to thinking that the way that she read said anything about who she might be to others. "Now I think about everything that I read when I was younger . . ." Jane said, trailing off. "It makes me angry."

"Do you know why you're angry?" I asked, uneasy.

"Well, yeah," she said, looking at me as if the answer were obvious. "I would have lived my life differently."

Reading a book is not an afternoon under the shade of a tree. It is splitting wood, hard work. Something is at stake for you. Reading is fighting. The greatest Chinese hero, Guan Yu, is usually depicted either getting ready to brawl or else reading, either a polearm or a book at the ready.

* * *

For me, learning how to be a good reader in this country, in the eyes of others and then in my own eyes, came at a cost too. In 1971, when we left Hong Kong, my mother packed a set of books in her suitcase along with her clothes and probably some dried food. They were kindergarten-level Chinese readers for my sister Selma, who in time came to dislike her English name, a homophone, despite its deep American connotation. My mother planned to use the readers with me too in time, but she quit Selma's lessons after only a few months and then gave up the idea of teaching us Chinese altogether. "Your father told me to stop," she explained. "He wanted you to play with the other kids." I wonder what happened in that brief time to change his mind. It's possible he had already committed to our assimilation before we departed, or maybe something or someone in this country made the difference. If so, I want it to be because he felt good, as he did when a stranger praised his English, before we knew to call it a "microaggression" and be done with it. Or it could have been a one-off, like a waitress refilling his coffee cup and winking at him after he said, "Thank you, miss." I want to think that he chose "Frederick" for his papers just to show he could pronounce it. Whatever the reason behind Dad's decision may have been, the line of our literacy in Chinese will likely end with my parents. I recognize only a few words of Chinese, although to earn a doctorate I had to prove that I could read two other foreign languages, one of them dead.

The lurking shame I feel about my illiteracy in Chinese is the opposite of the pride I held as a child knowing only English, when I was a native speaker, yes, but a native reader as well, my spine as upright as a book's on a shelf. Now in middle age, I wonder if it is too late for lessons. Then I would have Chinese, as well as fluent English, as a ward against judgment, if only to signal that I have other options and another people. I suppose this is how the truly devout must feel about their faith. Baldwin, who once spoke in tongues, found comfort in his church for a time and was invited by Elijah Muhammad to find it in another. I'll feel this way too and suffer the stares. It can be done if all I want is the confidence for ordering drinks and sealing deals, the Chinese of AP seniors and B-school hopefuls. Then there are the heritage classes, for those more like me, Chinese who arrived young or were the children of immigrants, for whom language is not a tool. I should expect to be the elder of the class, like Jane, and would have to muster her grace to see it through. But the identity angle is not quite right either, the textbook Mandarin being so alien from the Cantonese that still bleats in my head and can turn it on a busy American street. We would have to read to understand each other. But all this would feel wrong too, coveting a language because of shame, remaking myself based on what I feared others saw in me. I did that already, years ago. For now, I must be satisfied reading the way I have learned to read, which is in a language that this country has truly made its own, over time, most notably with its innocence.

Chinese may be better for reading the truth about our experiences in this country. Some Chinese people who wanted to become Americans did so by writing on walls. These people wrote poems, also stories about racism. Over the decades of the exclusion era, tens of thousands were held on Angel Island in San Francisco Bay, now a pleasant ferry ride from the mainland. The unluckiest were kept for months while officials vetted their claims to entry. Because only those among them who were born to US citizens could become American citizens, the trickier immigrants lied about the identity of their real fathers and claimed to be the sons of other Chinese men who were already citizens. They saved up and paid handsomely for this new identity, which included coaching books with the answers to the questions asked by examiners about their counterfeit families and homes in China. These immigrants were called "paper sons." Most were young men, teenagers with little schooling, but some of their poems followed the classical style. More than two hundred poems were carved into the barracks walls in Chinese calligraphy.

In 1970, a park ranger discovered the poems and saved the site from demolition. Their tone was usually remorseful and lonely, sometimes angry:

留筆除劍到美洲，
誰知到此淚雙流？
倘若得志成功日，
定斬胡人草不留 。

Leaving behind my writing brush and removing my sword,
I came to America.
Who was to know two streams of tears would
flow upon arriving here?
If there comes a day when I will have attained
my ambition and become successful,
I will certainly behead the barbarians and
spare not a single blade of grass.

Their stories bore no delusion or false innocence. Newcomers to Angel Island read themselves into the stories of those who had arrived before them, good readers from the outset. Those who weren't deported became Americans with poetry in their hearts.

CHAPTER 8
ELEVEN AND
A HALF POUNDS

On the wood paneling above the tabletop shrine in my parents' house are framed photos of my ancestors, the most recent addition being the self-portrait my father took for his passport but never used, the one I blew up on the computer before his funeral. It's the only one in color. His side of the family is more prominent on the wall than my mother's, which includes a man I have never met, her father. The face of my maternal grandfather is a cipher, not only because he died shortly after my mother learned she was pregnant with me, but because she rarely talked about him when I was a boy. He was involved in a mysterious scandal that my father sometimes brought up—always in Chinese—to shame her and win an argument. It usually worked. His memory never surfaced whenever my mother made us kids sit and visit with my grandmother, who came to live with us in Texas for a time until my father lost patience with her and insisted on her return to Hong Kong. The photo of my grandfather was taken in the fifties, a good decade for him, and shows a middle-aged man with a lean, oval face and half-rimmed Wayfarer-style eyeglasses, unsmiling, naturally, and wearing a suit and tie that somehow makes him appear more professional than my father, who chose the same look for his own photo. I always saw that photo of my grandfather in a more romantic light than those surrounding it because I imagined it being taken while he was on the job.

After my father died, I asked my mother to tell me more about her own father, who I knew was a detective in Hong Kong. She was more open to talking about the past now that she lived in the house alone. "He fell from grace," she began dramatically. She admitted that she didn't remember much about his career, only that it was a good one—certainly for a young immigrant like him from Guangdong Province—and on the rise before he was fired, which turned out to be the most forgiving of the possible outcomes. My grandfather had worked his way up from patrolman to detective. "He didn't have to wear a uniform. He could wear his regular clothes," my mother said. He belonged to what she called the "political" division. "Some of the people below him set him up. They were jealous of him." When the scandal broke, my mother was studying abroad at the University of Washington. "The police ransacked our apartment and read all the letters I had been sending home," she said. Apparently, the investigators accused him of taking bribes because he had the money to send his daughter to college in the States. But the letters revealed that my mother had gotten a job at Trader Vic's and didn't need her parents to send any money. "I was sending money to them," she said.

I wondered what it must have been like for a young Chinese man to go from fighting the Japanese to joining the ranks of a colonial institution like the Hong Kong Police Force. As a kid, I was proud that Hong Kong was a British colony, but now I hoped that my grandfather was an anti-imperialist at heart, investigating corruption within the force and perhaps even beyond, on up to the governor's office, building cases to implicate his British-born superiors. But none of that was true. My mother kept black-and-white snapshots that he had taken of himself with a tripod and remote shutter—fifties selfies—that showed him relaxing in his apartment: reading the newspaper, chatting on the phone, fiddling with his stereo, fixing a drink at his minibar. Far from being an anti-imperialist, he was most likely investigating Communist activity in the city. Perhaps he was getting close to the truth when he was betrayed by his fellow officers, who in turn accused him of being a sympathizer. The charges were so serious, he told my grandmother (who told my mother), that there was a strong chance he would be deported back to Dongguan in Guangdong Province. "If they send me back," he supposedly said, "the real Communists will gun me down." He was not deported. I want to believe that my mother's letters made the difference. Still, he lost his job, his pension, and a new flat he had recently purchased for the family. What was left of his reputation was savaged too. "Everyone knew," my mother said. "It was all in the papers."

* * *

In 2014, a Black man was shot and killed by a police officer in New York City only two days before a Black boy in Cleveland met the same end, a circumstance that may explain why Akai Gurley was sometimes lost among the names of other Black victims of such violence that year: Tamir Rice, Michael Brown, Tanisha Anderson, John Crawford, Eric Garner. No video surfaced of his last moments, no looping afterlife of his death, which made placing his name trickier amid the litany. Even photos of him were scarce by comparison, online but not iconic. If our memory of Akai Gurley lapses now, it may be for any of these reasons. But depending on our own needs, other details from the investigation of his homicide can keep his memory close. His life was taken by an act that so many, including me, could not rightly call murder but that was also no accident. The officer who killed him did not dodge indictment like Daniel Pantaleo, who choked Eric Garner, or Darren Wilson, who shot Michael Brown, but stood trial for his crime. The last time an NYPD officer had been convicted of a wrongful shooting was in 2005. But the name of Akai Gurley has stayed with me for a personal reason. It is because whenever I hear it, I do not immediately picture his face but that of the officer who killed him, not a white veteran like the others in the news but a young Chinese American man named Peter Liang.

On the night in question, Officer Liang and his partner, Shaun Landau, were working overtime in the Louis H. Pink Houses, a public housing project in Brooklyn. Both men were rookies, Liang on the job for less than two years. There had been recent reports of shootings and robberies in the Pink Houses, and the officers were conducting a "vertical patrol," which required them to sweep the hallways and stairwells floor by floor in search of criminal activity. They would work their way down from the eighth floor of the building at 2724 Linden Boulevard, which had two stairwells. Broken lighting rendered one of these completely dark; the officers chose to begin with it. Landau shined his flashlight through the window in the stairwell door. Liang unholstered his pistol and pointed it in front of him. Then, holding a flashlight in his free hand, he pushed the door open with his right shoulder. According to Landau, who traded his testimony for immunity, Liang stepped onto the landing of the stairwell and fired his gun. Following the shot, Landau said, he heard footsteps running down the stairwell. Liang returned to his partner in the eighth-floor hallway. "It went off by accident," he told Landau.

Akai Gurley, who was born in St. Thomas and was an immigrant like Liang's parents, had been visiting his companion Melissa Butler in the Pink Houses that night. Butler had been braiding Gurley's hair in the seventh-floor apartment she shared with family. She and Gurley left the apartment and waited several minutes for the elevator before deciding to use the stairs. Butler testified that after they entered the stairwell, she heard a gunshot and saw a flash of light. They raced down the stairs to the fifth-floor landing, where Gurley collapsed. Butler sought help on the floor below, where a neighbor followed her to the stairwell with a phone, relaying first aid instructions from an EMS dispatcher. By this time, approximately three minutes after the shot, Liang and Landau had made their way to Gurley but walked around his body to the landing below, joining the neighbor on the phone. It took Liang another three minutes to report that a man had been shot and call for an ambulance. Butler performed chest compressions on Gurley despite both officers having been trained in CPR and required to administer it. "He's not breathing," she screamed. Investigators later discovered that the round that killed Gurley had ricocheted off the wall of the stairwell, taking a terrible angle and tearing through his heart only inches away.

Until the day he was convicted of second-degree manslaughter, Peter Liang looked the same in almost every photograph I saw of him. He wore a white shirt under a black or gray suit, accented with a colorful tie. His ink-black hair was neatly clipped short, only an unruly cowlick making the difference between any two takes. He was usually caught in motion, in the process of being led somewhere, no doubt from the custody of one official to another. The low angle of the lens accentuated his build, like that of a strong safety, taller and more impressive than those of the white men escorting him. But it was his face that I found myself returning to, an infuriating blank mask except during those closing moments in the courtroom when it was not visible at all, cupped by his hands in grief. Others pausing upon his likeness may have seen it differently. They may have discerned, they supposed, a belated serenity that had settled upon it as his day in court approached. His aspect may have even struck some, against their better judgment, as characteristically Oriental in its equanimity. Yet what I saw in the unchanging face of Peter Liang was none of this.

The look I saw could belong only to an American like him and evinced, I have to think, nothing short of terror.

*   *   *

The aftermath of the shooting exposed deep political rifts among Chinese Americans, not only in New York but across the country. The most visible public assemblies were those backing Liang and claiming that the shooting was a "tragic accident" with "two victims." Liang, they implied, was a "scapegoat" for the unindicted white officers who had also killed unarmed Black men in recent months. As the filmmaker Ursula Liang (no relation) portrayed in her documentary *Down a Dark Stairwell*, activists from groups such as the Coalition of Asian Americans for Civil Rights (CAACR) used the Chinese social media platform WeChat to communicate with and organize tens of thousands of Chinese Americans from coast to coast. The Chinese government, seeing the case as another example of the United States' hypocrisy when blaming China for its own internal conflicts, reported on it in state media and permitted its citizens to follow it online on WeChat. Perhaps the largest protest occurred in February 2016, after Liang's conviction. A crowd estimated to be as large as ten thousand strong filled Brooklyn's Cadman Plaza Park to advocate for lenient sentencing. The CAACR announced that protests took place in forty-three cities and drew more than one hundred thousand people in total. A Chinese American postal worker who had been in the country for forty years said that it was the first protest he had attended in his life. Others held up signs that read NO SCAPEGOAT and, alongside a photo of MLK, INJUSTICE ANYWHERE IS A THREAT TO JUSTICE EVERYWHERE.

Asian Americans supporting the conviction and incarceration of Liang also took to the streets. Members of the Coalition Against Asian American Violence, for example, joined with other community organizers, including the loved ones of Akai Gurley, to bring the case within the scope of the Black Lives Matter movement. The public should not think of Liang as a Chinese American, they argued, still less a scapegoat because of it, but as part of a state institution that systematically targeted Black people. "He had no problem being part of the system until the system turned on him," said one woman in the days leading up to sentencing after Brooklyn district attorney Ken Thompson recommended no jail time for Liang. Diverse groups of protesters chanted and gripped signs that read JAIL KILLER COPS, often across the street from the mostly Chinese American crowds supporting Liang. Only two weeks after Liang killed Gurley, a Staten Island grand jury found no probable cause to indict Daniel Pantaleo, the NYPD officer whose chokehold had led Eric Garner to cry out for air. Pantaleo had received unwavering and full-throated support from his union and fellow officers, it seemed to me. In Wisconsin, far from the epicenter of both cases, I closely followed the protests on TV and social media, trying to understand the difference between them and what they might mean for Akai Gurley and Peter Liang.

I wanted Liang to go to jail. In the year of "I Can't Breathe" and "Hands Up, Don't Shoot," protest slogans drawn from the accounts of Eric Garner's and Michael Brown's deaths at the hands of police, it was even clearer to me that he should be indicted and convicted for his crime. I called for justice for Akai Gurley on social media, and I blogged about why Liang's Chinese American supporters were complicit in a racist system pitting them against Black Americans for the benefit of white supremacy. I was angry at Liang for thinking only about himself as Gurley lay dying. I could not excuse his failure to minister to the injured man in the ways that he had been trained to, a dereliction shared by his partner. More than anything, I was angry at him for being too scared to perform his sworn duty without endangering the lives of innocents. Likewise, I wanted an indictment of Daniel Pantaleo and Darren Wilson, who had claimed that their fear of Black men had justified their killing them. Liang should have gone to jail, but I cannot say that he belongs in the company of Pantaleo and Wilson, whose deadly force did not reveal their fear of the Black man so much as their contempt for him. Neither should he be in the company of Thomas Lane, J. Alexander Kueng, and Tou Thao, the Minneapolis police officers who, in 2020, stood by as their compatriot Derek Chauvin crushed the life from George Floyd, Thao an Asian American like Liang. Throughout Liang's trial, a premise that neither the prosecution nor the defense bothered to dispute was that Liang—instructed multiple times by Judge Danny Chun to speak louder—was scared. If there was anything I might know about Liang, it was that the depths of his fear, up to the point when he pulled the trigger, were largely unknown to him.

*   *   *

One could say that Liang and I had nothing in common except our race, as if it were possible for the reach of the word to end right there. If we were to meet today, he might tell me that I knew nothing about what it was like to be him, a patrol officer, and to experience the feel of a gun in your hand, knowing what it was used for. He might say that despite our common heritage, the futures fanning out before us as children were already divergent, which, as far as I can tell, would also be true. If he were in an especially cruel mood, he might add that I was hardly Chinese at all, there being no trace of Chinese language or filiality in the home I shared only with my wife and son. I would have nothing to say in answer to that. If we were to meet today, I might tell Liang that we two strangers did have a fundamental knowledge of each other. It had to do with how we had chosen to lead our lives despite being Chinese in this country, or, more accurately, despite knowing what the public made of that fact. What did it mean to be Asian like us and choose to serve that public as the guardians of its culture? I would ask him why he opted for a trial by jury instead of a trial by judge. Where did his faith in his peers come from? Did he really think that others wouldn't notice what was different about him, or that he knew their hearts better than they? Did he ever consider what failure might look like?

In 2022, the Justice Department ended a program called the China Initiative, an effort begun during the Trump administration to investigate Chinese researchers, especially those with appointments and affiliations with universities in the United States and China, for a host of alleged offenses that included espionage and cybercrime. Trump himself had said that China was "raping our country." According to Gideon Lewis-Kraus of the *New Yorker*, Trump reportedly added, "Almost every student that comes over to this country is a spy," referring to people from China. The Justice Department did secure convictions under the China Initiative, the most publicized being that of the Harvard chemist

Charles Lieber, who is not Chinese. Lieber was found guilty of lying about his participation in a Chinese recruitment program and failing to report income earned in China as well as the Chinese bank account where he kept it. Since its inception in 2018, the China Initiative has withdrawn multiple cases and lost others in court, the crime in question being not espionage or the exchange of trade secrets but a kind of fraud, namely the failure to disclose Chinese affiliations on federal grant proposals. Gang Chen, an engineering professor at MIT, had the case against him dropped after prosecutors learned that he was not required to disclose those affiliations, but the damage had already been done to his reputation and networks. Other Chinese scientists and professors in the United States have been put on leave or fired. A former FBI agent told Lewis-Kraus, "The F.B.I. will say, 'If you look at our cases, people of Chinese origin are overrepresented,' but that's not measuring spies—it's measuring who the F.B.I. is investigating."

Most people don't become professors for the money. I imagine the primary compensation is the soft promise of a purposeful life, one contributing to the greater good by asking questions about the unknown. My mother had been the parent most concerned about my career as a professor. Given the vicissitudes of her father's life and of our family business when I was growing up, she liked the idea of tenure when I mentioned it to her and didn't ask many questions about the reasons for it. She grasped that publishing was an important part of getting it, and she inquired if I was doing enough of it. Neither she nor my father knew what, exactly, I was supposed to write about, only that it had something to do with people like us. If I emailed an announcement with my name in it from our news bureau, I would find a streaky inkjet printout of it pinned to a bulletin board in my old room the next time I came home for Christmas. From these notices, my mother learned that my appointments revolved around campus diversity, so when we talked on the phone, she would ask plainly, "How is your die-versity going?" The question, I realize now, was related to her concern about my saying something controversial and getting into trouble for it. The word came to stand in for others—"civil rights," "anti-racism," "social justice"—that were more accurate but that she, like almost everyone else, either didn't know or didn't care to use if she did. "Don't say all those things about white people," she blurted out after she had just seen a news story about white supremacists. "The students have guns now," she added.

My parents were pleased that I took an interest in being Chinese, but they didn't see what it had to do with discrimination against Black people. Back then, I couldn't explain how our rights had been fought for by the Black Americans they didn't know and not gifted to us by the white Americans we did. As far as they could tell, it wasn't their problem. At a trade show in New Orleans, my father introduced me to a gregarious white woman who had voted for David Duke. Dad must have bragged to her that I was going to school to be a professor, at which point she began to speak to me like a teacher. I was twenty-one years old. She gestured at a booth across the aisle that sold cheap, mass-produced oil paintings. "That's General Robert E. Lee," she said, pointing at a huge portrait, probably painted in a factory in southern China. "He was a great man." The woman also didn't believe that discrimination was or should be my problem. At my parents' house and office, there were no portraits or photos of anyone but our family, which slowly included more white people over the years. If my mother could see my department building at the university, she would likely be puzzled by why grown adults like us professors would tack black-and-white postcards or posters of dead strangers on their walls—James Baldwin, Virginia Woolf, Karl Marx. What could home possibly mean, she might think, if sons and daughters saw themselves in this way? One difference between my parents and me was our willingness to feel a connection to a people who were not our own.

Many years ago, I taught a section of first-year writing intended to be more inclusive for people of color, perhaps because it was usually taught by one. I chose the course theme of race and racism in the United States. One of my students was a young Black woman who had just moved from the South Side of Chicago. We must have been talking about the model minority stereotype of Asian Americans, namely our celebrated penchant for education and law-fulness, and how the stereotype crystallized in the 1960s to turn public opinion against Black civil rights protesters, who supposedly had neither of these qualities. After class that day, she told me that she had grown up being told by her family to beware of the crime that pervaded their neighborhood. "If there isn't a lot of crime where I live," she asked me, "why are the police always there?" I asked her what she thought counted as a crime. Mostly drug dealing, she said. "You see a lot of police," I said, "because they think the people in your neighborhood are doing that more than the people in my neighborhood." The former FBI agent had said that Chinese professors were overrepresented in law enforcement actions too, which was to say only that you're the model minority until you're not.

There is an old photo of me with my students from this class in which everyone is smiling. The shot was hastily assembled, the twelve of us pulled together from those streaming out of a banquet ballroom. We had been toasting the successes of people of color like ourselves, winners of scholarships and appreciation awards. We were dressed up. The photo might bolster the claims of diversity researchers that a critical mass of people with something in common would make all the difference. Yet, despite our smiles, the best word to describe what we all had in common was "fear," although we did not feel fear at that moment we were smiling for the camera, or earlier at the ceremony, or very often in our class together. It was a fear of what we already knew about ourselves in the world, including even in this university that was willing to give us a chance, if only we would evidence that the generosity was not ours but theirs. It was neither a crippling nor ever-present fear, only one of being brought here for the benefit of others and not ourselves. It was the fear that the new home that we somehow found ourselves in was not ours at all because we were not white, and it was also the fear of the white people who knew and depended on our doubts without ever needing to acknowledge them.

*   *   *

The sin of Peter Liang was that he was afraid of the wrong thing. What made it worse for him was that everyone seemed to know it. The activists who condemned him and the police who might have supported him both knew it. Perhaps, eventually, he knew it too. A few days after the news broke of

Akai Gurley's death, St. Louis County released testimony from Darren Wilson's grand jury case, in which the officer said that he had feared for his life during his encounter with Michael Brown. Wilson compared Brown to "Hulk Hogan" and a "demon," adding that a "grunting" Brown charged toward him through a hail of gunfire and could have killed him with a single punch. In the week to follow, national publications were flooded with op-eds connecting Wilson's words to the racist stereotype of the invulnerable, brutish Black man. MICHAEL BROWN WASN'T A SUPERHUMAN DEMON, read the headline for Jamelle Bouie's column for *Slate*. Such a phantom may have lurked in the mind of Peter Liang as well. His fear of it lying in wait in a stairwell of the Pink Houses spoke to his failure of imagination as well as to his guilt. His fear had told him that a bullet, maybe more than one, was the only line of defense against such an opponent. I believe that Liang would have been acquitted if he could have testified that he had seen a real Black man in the stairwell. Even smug people who allege to be color-blind know that it is one thing to shoot at a body attached to an idea and another to shoot at an idea detached from a body.

The pressure of the stereotype on Liang was at least eleven and a half pounds. His pistol had what is called a "heavy trigger pull." Eleven and a half pounds is the exact amount of pressure required to fire it, more than twice the amount required for the same model that Glock released to the public. At the trial's turning point, to prove that Liang was in full control of his weapon and that it did not discharge accidentally, prosecutors passed the pistol around to jurors and asked them to try to pull the trigger themselves. At first some refused to do so. Before this moment, only ten of the twelve jurors were ready to convict Liang, who testified that his finger had been on the gun's frame, per regulation, not on the trigger. "We knew his testimony wasn't completely true," said Carlton Screen, the only Black juror. "It was very hard to pull the trigger." Liang testified that he had performed hundreds of vertical patrols and had drawn his gun because "there are bullet holes in the roof" and because "people get assaulted and raped in these areas." The prosecution could not speculate on the stereotype that Liang had been afraid of; he was not on trial for his beliefs but his actions. "And as soon as I got in, I heard something on my left side," Liang testified at his trial. "It was a quick sound, and it just startled me. The gun just went off." Because he could not admit that he had been scared by his belief in the idea of a violent Black man, Liang told jurors that he had been scared by a sound.

Liang claimed he never saw Gurley. Prosecutors painted Liang as a reckless man afraid to take responsibility for his actions. His partner, Shaun Landau, reminded him to notify a superior officer for discharging his weapon. "You call," Liang said. When the two finally reached Gurley, neither provided any aid. "Instead of doing all he could," said Brooklyn assistant district attorney Marc Fliedner, "Liang didn't call for help. He stood there whining and moaning." What did fellow officers say about Liang behind closed doors? What they said about him out in the open was telling enough. If only he could say that he had been scared by a person and not a sound, they might have gossiped, they could have backed him as they did Pantaleo and Wilson. Liang's story could have been one of innocence like theirs, that of an officer protecting his life from imminent peril— Eric Garner piggybacking Pantaleo toward a plate glass window or Michael Brown bull-rushing Wilson while reaching for his waistband. But the fact was that the evidence made it impossible for Liang to be afraid of Gurley, even though his claim of innocence needed him to be. Perhaps other officers even laughed or shook their heads at him in private for allowing himself to be afraid of the wrong thing in public. Because Liang's testimony had turned Gurley invisible in that stairwell, his story could not be one of innocence, only incompetence.

I wonder when Liang realized that he had been afraid of the wrong thing. Perhaps it was early in the investigation, when, in a rare move, the NYPD released the names of officer and victim one day after the shooting, Commissioner William Bratton referring to Gurley as "a total innocent." It could have been a few months before trial, when, unhappy with his representation, Liang dismissed his lawyer appointed by the Patrolmen's Benevolent Association (PBA) and hired a team funded by donations from the Chinese American community. Or maybe it was the first day of the trial, when the PBA, usually out in force at police misconduct trials, sent only two members in support. Or when, on a day when the PBA showed up in numbers, Shaun Landau testified that Liang had said, "I'm fired," moments after the shooting. Or when responding officer Lieutenant Vitaliy Zelikov said that Liang was "frozen" in the stairwell, unable to do police work or even stand on his own two feet before dropping to the hallway floor. It may have been when Liang found himself weeping openly on the stand, even turning his body to shield his face from the jury for minutes. Or the notion may have come to him as early as that night in the stairwell with Gurley. Without excusing his actions, or lack of them, it is fair to say that Liang was in shock at the time. If only in a flash, he may have seen that it was not the idea of a Black man he should fear but the racist society that had dreamed it. That revelation may have been followed by another, which was that that very same society had dreamed up an idea of him too.

A month after Liang was sentenced, WABC-TV Eye-witness News in New York aired a short segment on his whereabouts. EXCLUSIVE: SEE WHERE PETER LIANG IS CLEANING TOILETS, read the headline on the station's website. Liang was fired after his conviction but avoided any jail time, sentenced to five years of probation and eight hundred hours of community service on a reduced charge of criminally negligent homicide. Only at his sentencing did he apologize to the Gurley family and to Kimberly Ballinger, the mother of Gurley's young daughter. He would spend six months at a community center for Chinese American senior citizens, "mopping floors and serving meals to the elderly," in addition to cleaning toilets. Julia Kuan, an attorney advising the center, called the sentence "sort of a humbling experience" for Liang and said that she expected him to "gain something from it." How did New Yorkers who weren't Black or Asian measure such a penance? It may have been a feel-good story to some, and others may have snickered at the sight of a guilty cop brought low. Liang could have been happy to be unafraid for once, amid so many familiar faces. But maybe he also understood that the justice this country demanded from him was not his incarceration but his exile. After concluding his community service, Liang took a job at "a Chinese-owned warehouse in Brooklyn," the journalist

Marrian Zhou found, and "still lives at the family home, on the second floor, with his wife."

By all accounts, Liang was a good son. As newlyweds, he and his wife moved in with his parents. He lovingly inscribed birthday cards to his mother. When he became a police officer, he told her to retire, his salary enough to support them. He and his mother appeared at press conferences together, including the one at which she told reporters that her son had dreamed of being a police officer since he was five, when he saw two Black men rob her of a gold necklace. He was willing to take his defense as far as he needed to in order to return to his family. That included petitioning Judge Chun for a mistrial after it was discovered that a juror had lied about his history. His team began raising funds for an appeal until prosecutors threatened their own appeal of Chun's decision to reduce the original charge of manslaughter. Liang went as far as to turn his back on his department, it seemed, perhaps after feeling "abandoned by the government after serving as a police officer," as a family friend suggested. After changing his legal team, Liang took the stand and blamed his department and fellow officers for his inaction that night, claiming that he wasn't properly trained in CPR at the police academy and was given the answers on the written exam. Even if he had been acquitted, it was hard to see Liang returning to active duty with the full respect of his fellow officers. His family had to be enough.

* * *

"I remembered something I forgot to tell you earlier," Mom said the day after she told me about my grandfather's ejection from law enforcement. "I remember another police officer would come to our apartment at night, and I would see him giving my father a bundle of cash." This was before my grandfather was fired. I asked if she thought her father was taking bribes, either from Communist agents or from organized crime. "It wasn't a bribe. I think the money was for paying people for information," she replied. "It was for informants." My mother needed to believe that the money was not a bribe. I think she may not have been exactly right when describing my grandfather's fate as a fall from grace, but it was certainly a fall. So much of his life seemed to leave him in an instant. He was forsaken by his former colleagues and even some family. He pleaded with his brother-in-law for an entry-level job at his convenience store but couldn't secure even that. His son, my uncle Robert, a teenager at the time of the scandal, was bullied at school. My grandfather wasn't without fault in other parts of his life. He had been a "womanizer"—my mother's word—all his life. He had married my grandmother but then also married her sister, installing himself at the head of parallel households that he now had no means to support. My mother had two half sisters who were also her cousins. I asked if she was close to them, desperately wanting a silver lining. "No, not really," she said. "Although the younger one let me baptize her." There was also a mistress. Not six years after he was fired, my grandfather was dead.

I won't ever know the whole story about him. I'd like to think that he told the truth and paid the price for it, betrayed by ambitious and corrupt underlings. But maybe he did accept a bribe every now and then, from the man in the shadows or not. So many civil servants in Hong Kong were on the take at the time; even nurses expected a little something for their trouble, I've heard. By the time my mother told me what she knew, I was already fifty-one, the age that my grandfather was when he lost his job. He had held it since 1946, after the Hong Kong Police Force was returned to civil administration following years under Japanese rule. The institution was rebuilding from scratch, and he was getting in on the ground floor. While beginning the process of granting independence to its other possessions after the war, Britain decided not only to keep Hong Kong as a crown colony but to showcase it as a jewel of Western influence in Asia during the Cold War. As a patrolman, my grandfather probably dealt firsthand with the refugee crisis that started even before Mao declared victory. The population of Hong Kong jumped from fewer than eight hundred thousand in 1945 to three million in 1960. The prisons filled up. In 1956, a riot broke out among newly resettled refugees in a shoddy government housing project. More than six thousand refugees were arrested and fifty-nine died, most of them killed by the police, I assume. I wonder how my grandfather saw these people, some of whom he could have known back in Dongguan. Did he see himself as being more like them or more like his fellow officers, so many of whom, imported from overseas territories like Palestine, were white like their superiors on up to the commissioner?

I doubt that my grandfather was a Communist, either a sympathizer or a spy. He was terrified of being deported and maybe executed, according to my grandmother. And perhaps it was because she hated him that she liked to revive the memory of his fear again and again for herself and her only daughter. On top of that, the motivations of the man I saw in the snapshots were transparent; that man was happy with the middle-class life he had made for himself in the colony and was unafraid of the future. In fact, he may have just stopped wondering if his new life could ever possibly go away. I couldn't really blame him. He probably didn't expect to climb as rapidly as he did and then find himself in a position of authority as well. If he was made a scapegoat, it was because he was an easier target as an immigrant, a Chinese man, or both.

* * *

It made sense that my grandfather's life was as complex and troubled as the Hong Kong that he had wanted for himself. He could have been a patsy *and* an agent. What too many of the activists on either side of Peter Liang ignored, I think, was that he was never only a convenient scapegoat or a tool of oppression. Not only could he play both roles, but as an Asian American he was particularly well suited to do so, given how often the meaning of our race changes. Liang simply became what each side needed him to be. For the Chinese government, he became a symbol of a double standard in reporting on human rights abuses that predictably cast China as the villain, with the United States as the moral authority. For his Chinese American supporters, Liang metonymized hot-button issues like affirmative action, which also did not see Asians as possible victims of racial discrimination. The WeChat platform connected both these groups. To his detractors, there was no way to isolate the case from the relentless flood of stories of Black lives taken by police violence. Liang had chosen to become a police officer even though he had already held a stable civil service job.

He had chosen to draw his gun. In America, there was no doubt that Liang benefited from not being Black, but that was not the same as being white. Whether you bore the sins of others or enabled them depended on how well you knew your own fears at any given moment.

"I thought of another story to tell you," Mom said out of the blue one afternoon. "I don't know what made me think of it. Do you remember we used to go to Montgomery Ward? It was a department store. It's gone now."

"I remember it."

"I had to go there one day. We were living in the apartment in Dallas. You were little," she said. "I was in the parking lot of the mall, looking for a space, and I must have cut off this other driver."

"Was I there?"

"No, I was by myself. This guy was so mad at me. He yelled at me. Cursed me."

"Was he white?"

"Yes, he was white. I bet he didn't think I could speak English. I yelled right back at him. Told him not to talk to me that way. I think he was surprised I did that."

I laughed and said that I was proud of her. But I also told her not to do that anymore. "A Chinese woman was set on fire in New York," I said.

It happened in Bensonhurst, Peter Liang's neighborhood. Two men assaulted an eighty-nine-year-old Chinese woman on the street, slapping her face and lighting her clothes on fire. Her pink seersucker shirt looked like something my mother might wear. The woman didn't tell her family until the next morning because she didn't want to worry them. It had been a few years since my mother had asked about my job by calling it my "die-versity" and telling me to be careful. Now I had to worry. Lately we had been reserving a few minutes of our conversations to talk politics, including how Donald Trump was making things worse for Chinese people like us. My parents voted in only one presidential election—Reagan in 1980. After one of my parents was called to jury duty the next year, neither one voted again. "We couldn't take time off from our business," Mom explained. They were like the immigrants in New York City's Chinatown who couldn't afford a day to rally outside of the courthouse for Liang. But my father was tapped as a juror after Texas switched to using driver registrations instead of voter rolls for selection. "He tried to get out of it by telling them that he thought defendants were usually guilty," Mom said. "They still picked him."

It was the classic Chinese ethic that everyone knew, certainly Peter Liang, and even those who weren't Chinese but only watched movies, that of loyalty to the needs of your family first, even before those of your country. It must be why so many immigrants, not only Chinese, decide to cross borders once they find a way. Only when my mother began to tell me about her father did I realize how little she had seen of him herself, the distance between them spooling out for her at the same age I was when I left home. She traveled farther for school than I had, to another land altogether, also thinking she might become a teacher. By the time she returned to Hong Kong to get married, my grandfather had already left my grandmother. He split his time between his second wife and his mistress, who was supporting him, before a stroke finally killed him at fifty-eight, a year before I was born. He died in an ambulance en route to the hospital. My mother didn't get a chance to say goodbye to her father either. Like her mother, she must have resented him, not as much or in the same way, but there had to come a point when she was forced to accept that their family was not going to be enough for him. From the opposite generation, I've put her in the same position, not for the same reasons but because of the same tendencies, outward, all the men in her life sojourners save one, who always returned home except for the last time.

My grandfather and Peter Liang both sought purpose in the folds of the state, which abided their presence until it became convenient to let them go. They were the dreamed but never the dreamers. I don't know whether my grandfather ever felt that he had anything in common with the desperate refugees streaming over the border or even with the agents priming their exodus, the Reds who may have murmured that he might be a hero to the people and not an imperialist stooge. Probably he didn't feel that connection, or not enough, seduced by the latest technology and the oldest temptation. What was or is in Peter Liang's heart will also remain a mystery to me, although I have conjectured what may have been in his head. That lie about a Black man in the dark, that dream, is our sorry inheritance as Americans. Even if we rebuke it, its trace lingers to haunt us, personalized, like a letter.

There are so many kinds of dreams meant to tell us who we are in this country. My father believed in the American dream for a time, and my mother warned me about my convictions because she hoped that dream might be mine still. Yet our most recent chats tell me that she now understands that it must belong to more than just our own to be real. Until that happens, the dream is merely a hallucination. Over my life, I have been given the benefit of the doubt and the means to become the dreamer too, a state of mind that can be a dismal oblivion, I learned. It was a place I had to leave. The dream is the problem that connects us all.

Acknowledgments

This book would not have been possible without the sharp eye and tireless dedication of my agent, Laura Usselman, of the Stuart Krichevsky Literary Agency, whose belief in me led us to the idea that became *Chinese Prodigal*. My deep gratitude goes to my editor at Grove Atlantic, Amy Hundley, for taking a chance on my story and pushing me to remain faithful to its purpose. I would not be nearly as proud of this book if not for the tremendous assistance of the team at Grove Atlantic, including Joseph Payne, who always brought good cheer and news my way, and Alicia Burns, who proofread the manuscript with skills I revere and envy.

I am indebted to my teachers who told me the truth about myself and the world that we shared. Garrett Hongo taught me that there were Asian Americans who wrote books, and that I might be one of them. Stephen Sumida taught me how to read those books and how to share the knowledge I made of them. There are so many others whose lessons remain with me still, including Señora Stacy, Elizabeth Harris, Sheldon Ekland-Olson, Tracy Daugherty, Diana Abu-Jaber, Sandra Gunning, Alan Wald, and Marlon Ross.

The University of Wisconsin–Eau Claire has been my academic home for over two decades. For their support, I am grateful to the Department of English, the College of Arts and Sciences, the College of Education and Health Sciences, the Office of Research and Sponsored Programs, and the University Research and Creative Activity Council. My thanks to colleagues past and present for their encouragement and ideas that found their way into my heart and this book, especially to Marty Wood, Susan Turell, Don Christian, Joel Pace, Erica Benson, Allyson Loomis, Osonye Tess Onwueme, Deb Barker, Asha Sen, Ari Anand, B. J. Hollars, Christina Wyman, Max Garland, Dorothy Chan, Tamara Johnson, José Alvergue, Bibiana Fuentes, Gerardo Licón, Blake Westerlund, Stephanie Farrar, Sarita Mizin, Stacy Thompson, and John Hildebrand.

Day in and day out, my students continue to make my job as fulfilling as I had hoped it would be as a young professor, and I am inspired by their capacity for change and justice. I especially want to recognize my Hmong American students for their grace and generosity in teaching me about the fullness of Asian American identity.

Many organizations and institutions provided a forum that allowed me to refine the ideas in *Chinese Prodigal*, including the Chippewa Valley Writers Guild; the ACLU of Wisconsin and its Chippewa Valley chapter; the Common Council of the City of Madison, Wisconsin; the *New York Times*; NPR's *Code Switch*; AsAmNews; *Reappropriate.co*; *Inside Higher Ed*; *Volume One* magazine; Adler University; the US Coast Guard Academy; and Stanford University's Arcade.

To those considerate souls whom I have met only online but who have encouraged my writing or answered the odd question out of the blue, I salute you, notably Juleyka Lantigua-Williams, Renee Tajima-Peña, Roland Greene, Randall Yip, Meredith Talusen, Sherrilyn Ifill, Jenn Fang, Ursula Liang, Estelle Grosso and Kino Lorber Inc., Curtis Chin, Jay Caspian Kang, Michael Solomon, Nikole Hannah-Jones, Jeff Yang, and Michael Eric Dyson.

My abiding affection goes out to friends who have inspired my writing life in one way or another—even before I had one—including Todd White, Scott Olson, Bill Grady, Chang-rae Lee, Michael Waite, Anne Heffron, Ryan Iwanaga, Erdağ Göknar, Catherine Paul, Brian Komei-Dempster, Jason Chu, Ian Leong, Rashied Robinson, Keith Lawrence, and Kao Kalia Yang.

None of this would have been possible without my wife, Robin, whose love and support have meant everything, those meanings now taken in the truest and healthiest sense by me. Our son, Jacob, is far in advance of where I was at his age, above all in his sense of right and wrong, as I like to tell him, but also in height, as he likes to tell me. For her enduring prayers, my gratitude goes to my sister-in-law, Alison. Only my best wishes to my mother-in-law, Mary Ann Richards, who, though not Chinese, also asks if I have eaten. To my father-in-law, Jacob P. Richards V, I hope the day is all fairways and greens.

Barriers of time and language distanced me from my grandparents, Shih Chih-Ming, Lee Shu-Hing, Chu Leung, and Ho Lai-Ching, so I weave our stories together now. All my love to my sisters, Selma Buehler and Teresa Downum, and their husbands, Alan and Brandon, as well as to my nieces and nephews, Emily, Allison, Joseph, Nicholas, Zachary, Aiden, and Liam. My mother, Violet, at once the least prodigal and most generous person I know, is the anchor of our family and always has been. At last, I offer up this paper of mine to my father, Frederick, who never refused any of my requests, extravagant or necessary, and whom I miss dearly.